THE COMPLETE

HIRING
AND
FIRING
HANDBOOK

Every Manager's Guide to Working with Employees—Legally

By Charles H. Fleischer
Attorney at Law

SPHINX® PUBLISHING
AN IMPRINT OF SOURCEBOOKS, INC.®
NAPERVILLE, ILLINOIS
www.SphinxLegal.com

First Edition: 2005

Published by: **Sphinx® Publishing, An Imprint of Sourcebooks, Inc.®**

<u>Naperville Office</u>
P.O. Box 4410
Naperville, Illinois 60567-4410
630-961-3900
Fax: 630-961-2168
www.sourcebooks.com
www.SphinxLegal.com

This publication is designed to provide accurate and authoritative information in regard to the subject matter covered. It is sold with the understanding that the publisher is not engaged in rendering legal, accounting, or other professional service. If legal advice or other expert assistance is required, the services of a competent professional person should be sought.

From a Declaration of Principles Jointly Adopted by a Committee of the
American Bar Association and a Committee of Publishers and Associations
This product is not a substitute for legal advice.
Disclaimer required by Texas statutes.

Library of Congress Cataloging-in-Publication Data
Fleischer, Charles H.
   The complete hiring and firing handbook : every manager's guide to working with employees legally / by Charles H. Fleischer.-- 1st ed.
       p. cm.
   Includes bibliographical references.
   ISBN 1-57248-458-6 (pbk. : alk. paper)
   1. Personnel management--Handbooks, manuals, etc. 2. Employee selection--Handbooks, manuals, etc. 3. Employees--Dismissal of--Handbooks, manuals, etc. I. Title.

HF5549.17.F58 2004
658.3'11--dc22

                                                                    2005022919

Printed and bound in the United State of America.
BG — 10 9 8 7 6 5 4 3 2 1

Contents

Introduction

The workplace is littered with legal land mines just waiting for an employer's misstep. Two of the really hot spots are hiring and firing. While every employment decision or personnel action carries some risk, perhaps at no other time is an employer exposed to such real danger as when bringing on a new worker or letting one go.

References to minefields are, of course, metaphorical. In fact, the real risk facing employers is being sued. Compared to a lawsuit, negotiating a minefield might almost be preferable.

Why is a lawsuit so hazardous? For one thing, it is extremely costly. In most of our major urban areas, defense attorneys charge several hundred dollars an hour. An employer who gets sued for age discrimination (as an example) can be almost certain of incurring thousands of dollars in legal fees, at a minimum. If the case involves complicated factual issues and statistical evidence, the eventual tab for fees, depositions, and expert witnesses can easily go much higher. And that's if you *win*! If you *lose*, add to that a jury verdict for back-pay, frontpay, compensatory damages, and punitive damages. You may also have to reimburse your former employee for his or her own legal fees.

Even if you had the foresight to purchase *Employment Practices Liability Insurance* (EPLI) to cover some of the costs of a lawsuit, lawsuits are hazardous in other ways. There's the disruption of answering written interrogatories, producing boxes of business records, and having half your workforce away at depositions instead of doing their jobs. This process, known as *discovery*, can go on for months.

Lawsuits are also public events. Anyone can go to the courthouse, pull the case file, and read all about your business practices, your employment procedures, your wage structure, and perhaps even your financial condition. Finally, there's the emotional cost of worrying about the suit, evaluating settlement demands, giving testimony in an unfamiliar, often hostile environment, and providing status reports to your directors or shareholders.

You may believe that mandatory *arbitration* is the answer. Arbitration may be cheaper, but is not necessarily so. Arbitrators charge substantial fees compared to judges, who are provided at taxpayers expense. Arbitration may also be quicker, but as arbitration becomes more formalized, with its own set of rules and procedures, the speed factor becomes less significant. Privacy is an advantage of arbitration, but at a price. Arbitrators can (and sometimes do) act *arbitrarily*, without giving reasons for their decisions, and with no accountability to the public or the appellate courts.

Finally, arbitration is frequently preceded by a lawsuit attacking the arbitration agreement as invalid or questioning whether the particular dispute falls within the terms of the agreement. So by having mandatory arbitration agreements with their employees, employers sometimes end up defending both a lawsuit *and* an arbitration claim.

EPLI coverage and mandatory arbitration may help, but they certainly do not eliminate all workplace legal hazards. Employers need to have policies and procedures in place that make adverse claims less likely in the first place. It is almost always better to avoid a lawsuit than to win one.

The goal of this book is to point out where the dangers lurk in the hiring and firing mine fields, and to guide you along the safest path. Others have come your way and left footprints. This book helps you follow them.

Disclaimer—*While every attempt has been made to provide accurate, authoritative, and current information regarding the subject matter covered, this book is for general information only and is not intended as legal or other professional advice. The reader should consult an attorney, accountant, or other appropriate professional regarding specific questions or problems. Neither the author nor the publisher is liable for any errors or omissions.*

This book contains links to third-party websites. Website addresses are subject to frequent change and over time may no longer work as intended. Neither the author nor the publisher is responsible for the functioning or content of any third-party website.

Part I

Hiring

To Hire or Not to Hire

Your business is booming. In fact, you have so much work in the pipeline that you are unable to fill orders as promptly as you would like. Customers are already complaining, and there is a real concern that you will lose some of them. Is it time to hire more staff?

Bringing on a new employee has certain advantages. For one, the employer has the right to *control* its employees. It is this very right of control that usually distinguishes *employees* from other types of workers, such as *independent contractors*. Further, having a staff of full-time, long-term employees promotes workplace stability in important ways. As employees build longevity, they hone their skills, they become familiar with the company culture, and, if treated well, they invest their efforts and loyalty in their work. In short, they identify with and think of themselves as part of the company.

There may also be tax advantages in hiring certain employees. In addition to allowing deductions for most wages and benefits, the Internal Revenue Code has long provided incentives for employing the disadvantaged. One current program is the *Empowerment Zone Employment Credit*. This program allows an employer to take a credit of up to $3,000 per year for wages paid to persons who live and work in an empowerment zone. This and other credits are explained more fully in IRS Publication 954, available at **www.irs.gov**.

States have a variety of tax credits as well. More information can be obtained from the *State Employment Security Agencies* (SESAs) listed in Appendix A.

There are also disadvantages in hiring. Not only will the employer have to pay wages, there are also payroll taxes and expenses—such as FICA, workers' compensation premiums, and unemployment insurance contributions—and benefits under group health, disability, and retirement plans. Payroll taxes and expenses can easily amount to 25% or more of basic wages.

Another disadvantage to hiring is the need for additional space to house the new employee and additional equipment to enable him or her to function. Computer workstations may be falling in price, but they are not free. The network may also have to be upgraded to accommodate the new employee, and additional software licenses may have to be purchased.

New employees need supervision and they place additional burdens on support staff, such as human resources and information technology personnel. The hiring process itself takes time and exposes the employer to claims of discrimination, anti-union animus, and the like.

Staying Small

If you are a small organization with few existing employees, expanding your workforce could push you over one or more statutory thresholds, subjecting you to additional legal requirements that may not otherwise be applicable. Expansion could also expose you to larger damage awards in discrimination cases. Many federal and state laws relating to the workplace have built-in floors based on the number of employees on your payroll. If you fall below the specified number, you are not subject to that law.

At the federal level, examples include:

- *Title VII of the Civil Rights Act*—15 or more employees;
- *Americans with Disabilities Act* (ADA)—15 or more employees;

◆ *Age Discrimination in Employment Act* (ADEA)—20 or more
  employees;

◆ *Consolidated Omnibus Budget Reconciliation Act* (COBRA)—
  20 or more employees;

◆ *Family and Medical Leave Act* (FMLA)—50 or more employees;
  and,

◆ *Worker Adjustment and Retraining Notification Act* (WARN)—
  100 or more employees.

Falling below a federal threshold does not necessarily mean you are free to
discriminate or to ignore health continuation or family leave obligations. State
and local jurisdictions often have their own laws containing prohibitions and
requirements similar to those in federal law, but with lower thresholds.

Alternatives to Hiring

Various alternatives to hiring may be attractive in given cases, but they have
their own disadvantages.

Overtime

One alternative is to require existing staff to work *overtime*. For employees
who do not fall within an exemption to the federal *Fair Labor Standards Act*
(FLSA) and within an exemption to state wage-and-hour laws, this generally
means paying the employees time-and-a-half for every hour they work in
excess of 40 hours in a given workweek. While some employees like overtime,
others do not, or they may have family or other commitments that prevent
them from working overtime.

The impact of the U.S. Department of Labor's (DOL) new rules for the
white collar exemptions from overtime (the exemptions for executives, administrators, professionals, and outside salespersons) is unclear at the time of this
writing. DOL claims that *more* employees will now be nonexempt and entitled

to overtime for work in excess of 40 hours-per-week, while others contend that fewer employees will get overtime under the new rules.

Regardless of their impact, the new overtime rules are clearer and simpler, so that an employer who is considering using overtime as an alternative to hiring more employees should have an easier time comparing the relative costs. (More information about the new rules is available from DOL at **www.dol.gov/esa/regs/compliance/whd/fairpay/main.htm**.)

Independent Contractors

Another alternative is to engage an *independent contractor*. True independent contractors are paid fees for their services and are issued IRS 1099 forms at year's end for tax purposes, but the employer has none of the other obligations associated with employees. For example, the employer does not have to withhold income tax or FICA; the employer has no matching FICA obligation; the employer does not face added workers' compensation premiums; and the employer does not have to include independent contractors in any benefit plans. Even most discrimination laws are inapplicable to independent contractors.

The danger of classifying a worker as an independent contractor, however, is that the classification may be wrong. If that happens, the employer will have retroactive liability to the IRS, state taxing authorities, workers' compensation insurers, and unemployment insurance departments.

Traditionally, the question whether a worker is an employee or an independent contractor turns on whether the employer has a right to control the manner in which the worker does his or her job. This is sometimes known as the *common-law test*. To determine whether there is or is not a right of control, a number of subsidiary factors are considered. These include:

- who sets the worker's hours;
- whether the worker works for one or several employers;
- whether the worker or the employer provides necessary tools and workspace; and,

◆ whether the worker has specialized knowledge or requires a
   license or a professional degree to do his or her job.

The IRS, for example, uses multiple factors in considering whether a worker
has been properly classified. (For more information on the IRS's classification
methodology, see Publication 15 [also known as Circular E] and Publication
15A, both available at **www.irs.gov**.)

Safe Harbor

The problem with the common-law test and the IRS's multi-factor approach
is their lack of certainty. In an effort to resolve this uncertainty, Congress
enacted legislation to provide a *safe harbor* for employers. Under these safe
harbor provisions, an employer's treatment of a worker as an independent contractor is relatively safe from IRS challenge, if:

   ◆ the employer has never treated the worker as an employee;
   ◆ the employer filed all required tax reports and returns relating
      to the worker on a timely and consistent basis; and,
   ◆ the employer had a reasonable basis for treating the worker as
      an independent contractor.

The employer will be considered as having a reasonable basis to treat the
worker as an independent contractor if the employer relied on a court decision
involving facts similar to its own, or if it relied on rulings or technical advice
from the IRS. The employer can also demonstrate a reasonable basis if a *significant segment of the industry* in which the worker is engaged has a long-standing, recognized practice of treating such workers as independent contractors.
A significant segment of the industry is 25%. However, the employer *will not*
have a reasonable basis for treating a particular worker as an independent contractor if the employer has other workers doing similar jobs who are treated as
employees.

While the IRS can still challenge a safe harbor classification, the burden of proving the classification wrong falls on the IRS. In order to ensure that the safe harbor provisions are fully effective, the IRS must provide the employer with a written notice of the provisions when it audits an employer in connection with a worker-classification issue. The IRS is also prohibited from issuing regulations or rulings dealing with the safe harbor provisions.

> ### Example
> A company licensed as a residential service agency in Maryland provided nonskilled, home health aides for the elderly. Before opening for business, the company conducted a survey of some twenty to thirty competitors in the Washington, D.C. metropolitan area. It found that approximately 80% of the agencies surveyed treated their workers as independent contractors, while only 10% treated them as employees. The other 10% did not respond. When the company decided to open additional offices in Baltimore and Richmond, it conducted similar surveys in those areas and obtained similar results. Based on these surveys, the company classified its workers as independent contractors. The court ruled that the company's reliance on its surveys was reasonable and that the company's classification of its aides was correct.
>
> *Options for Senior America Corp. v. United States, 11 F. Supp. 2d 666 (D.Md. 1998)*

Another approach to resolving the employee versus independent contractor problem for federal tax and withholding purposes is to ask the IRS to decide. On filing Form SS-8 (either by the employer or by the worker whose status is in doubt), the IRS will determine whether the worker is an employee or an independent contractor. The determination can then be relied on for safe harbor purposes. Of course, it is probably fair to assume that the IRS resolves close questions by concluding that the worker is an employee, not an independent contractor. As a practical matter, the SS-8 route may not be very helpful to employers.

Outsourcing Employees

Instead of hiring employees, you could *lease* them from a temp agency. Leasing is an ideal solution for short-term projects or unexpected increases in workload. A good temp agency will have screened the workers it offers, performed background checks, and perhaps even done skills testing. If the worker is unsatisfactory, it is easy enough to ask the temp agency for a replacement. Leasing also provides a relatively risk-free opportunity to evaluate a potential candidate for regular employment. The frequent leasing of employees may not be satisfactory on a long-term basis, since leased employees often do not have the job commitment and company loyalty that most employers want.

Leased employees are usually not considered part of your regular workforce. Therefore, they do not participate in your retirement or other benefit plans and they do not increase payroll expenses. On the other hand, the temp agency will have its own payroll expenses and profit margin, which are reflected in the hourly rate the agency charges for its workers.

Employee leasing is definitely *not* a technique to avoid workplace discrimination rules. It is just as illegal, for example, for a company to tell its temp agency to send only females for secretarial positions as it is for the company itself to reject all male candidates as secretaries. The federal civil rights laws do not only prohibit an employer from discriminating against its own employees—they also prohibit an employer from interfering with an individual's employment opportunities *with another employer*.

Example

A temp agency assigns one of its technicians to maintain and repair computers for a small, twelve-employee company. The agency supplies all the tools and direction for the repairs. The technician is present at the company's offices sporadically over a three-week period, working independently while there. The company has no authority to make assignments or require work to be done at particular times. After a few

(continued)

> visits, the company asks the agency to assign someone else, stating that it is not satisfied with the technician's repair skills. However, the real reason for the company's action is racial bias. As a result, the company is guilty of illegal discrimination.
>
> *EEOC Enforcement Guidance: Application of EEO Laws to Contingent Workers Placed by Temporary Employment Agencies and Other Staffing Firms (Dec. 3, 1997)*

In this example, the company is not the technician's employer because it does not have a right to control the technician's work. In fact, because the company falls below the fifteen-employee threshold specified in *Title VII* of the federal *Civil Rights Act*, it would not have violated *Title VII* if it had discriminated directly against the technician by refusing to hire him or her based on race. Yet, by asking the agency to assign someone else, the company interfered with the technician's employment opportunities with another employer—the temp agency—and is therefore in violation of *Title VII*.

Professional Employer Organizations

Instead of leasing employees from a temp agency, some employers have contracted with *Professional Employer Organizations* (PEOs) to provide HR-related functions for their employees. Those functions may include:

- payroll administration;
- workers' compensation administration;
- leave tracking;
- job analysis and job description services;
- advertising and recruitment strategies;
- background and reference checking;
- employee training courses (safety, nondiscrimination, etc.);
- termination guidance and services;
- benefit plan design and administration (401(k) plans, health insurance, cafeteria plans, etc.);

- wage garnishment management; and,
- COBRA and HIPAA compliance.

In a typical PEO arrangement, employees are considered *jointly employed* by both the PEO and the worksite employer, based on a lengthy written contract that spells out in detail the parties' respective responsibilities and liabilities. Any employer considering the PEO option will want to review the contract with great care and arrive at a thorough understanding of just how the relationship works. The PEO should also be able to provide a comparative cost analysis showing if the arrangement will in fact be a financial benefit. Finally, the employer should satisfy itself as to the PEO's integrity, experience, and financial standing before signing on.

Through economies of scale, PEOs may well be more cost-effective and efficient in providing employment-related services than some smaller, individual employers. (More information about PEOs is available from the National Association of Professional Employer Organizations at **www.napeo.org**.)

Outsourcing Work

Outsourcing some discrete portion of your work to a contractor can relieve burdens on existing staff, but there are drawbacks. For one, you lose control over the quality and timeliness of the work. If you are unionized, your union may insist that you bargain over the decision. And the contractor to whom you have outsourced the work may see an opportunity to pirate your customers. Finally, by outsourcing, your contractor enjoys any profits you would have made had you kept the work in-house. Outsourcing may be reasonable for work you cannot do efficiently or work you no longer wish to do, but it is hardly a prescription for growth.

2

Eligibility for Employment

Once you have made the decision to hire, you must consider who should be included and excluded from the pool of potential candidates. Some factors cannot be used to exclude, such as race, color, or other discriminatory criteria. (see Chapter 4.) Other factors may, or in certain cases must, be used to exclude candidates. These factors are covered in this chapter.

Child Labor

Both federal and state laws regulate child labor. On the federal side, the *Fair Labor Standards Act* (FLSA) prohibits *oppressive child labor*, which is defined as:

- employment of any child who is under the age of 16, regardless of the occupation and
- employment of a child who is between the ages of 16 and 18 in mining, manufacturing, or any other industry the Secretary of Labor finds particularly hazardous.

Excluded from the definition is:

- employment in a family business, so long as the employment is not in mining, manufacturing, or other particularly hazardous industries;

- agricultural employment (with parental consent if the child is under age 14, and only when school is not in session if the child is under age 16);
- employment as an actor or performer in movies, the theater, and radio and television productions;
- delivering newspapers to consumers; and,
- making wreaths at home and harvesting forest products to be used in wreath-making.

Separate federal legislation prohibits the employment of children in the production of child pornography for distribution in interstate commerce.

State regulation of child labor differs from jurisdiction to jurisdiction. The definition of *minor* may vary, for example. And each state also has its own list of favored exclusions, reflective of prominent local industries or regional customs. Specific work, such as serving alcoholic beverages or driving commercial vehicles, may be subject to additional age restrictions.

Minors need a work permit, typically issued through the school system, before being able to work. Employers must keep permits on file and available for inspection. Even when a minor is properly permitted to work, additional restrictions may apply, such as when and how many hours a minor may work. These time restrictions vary depending on whether school is or is not in session.

The illegal employment of minors exposes the employer to substantial criminal and civil penalties. In general, most businesses will restrict their candidate pool to persons 18 years-of age or older.

Foreign Workers

Since 1986, when the *Immigration Reform and Control Act* (IRCA) was passed, it has been illegal to knowingly hire, recruit, refer for a fee, or continue to employ persons who are not eligible to work in the United States.

Violation of the IRCA is a federal crime. Government contractors who violate the IRCA are subject to debarment. In addition, violators may be exposed to civil liability under the *Racketeer Influenced and Corrupt Organizations Act* (RICO).

> **Example**
>
> A cleaning company doing business in Connecticut was accused of hiring undocumented aliens for its business. The company was sued by one of its competitors on the basis that by engaging in a pattern of illegal hiring, the company reduced its labor costs and was able to underbid its competition. A federal court of appeals ruled that the suit, based on RICO, could go forward.
>
> *Commercial Cleaning Services, LLC v. Colin Service Sys., Inc., 271 F.3d 374 (2nd Cir. 2001)*

Work Visas

The immigration laws authorize a number of categories of nonimmigrant (temporary) work visas. These include:

- ◆ *H-1B*, for foreign professionals;
- ◆ *H-2B*, for foreign skilled and unskilled workers; and,
- ◆ *TN*, for Canadian and Mexican professionals.

General information about nonimmigrant (temporary) visas is available from the State Department's website at **http://travel.state.gov/visa/tempvisitors.html**. Information is also available from the United States Citizenship and Immigration Services, a bureau of the Department of Homeland Security, at **http://uscis.gov**.

H-1B Visas

H-1B visas allow foreign *specialty workers* (persons whose professions require at least a bachelor's degree or equivalent) to be employed in the U.S. for an initial three-year period, renewable for an additional three years. If the particular field of work also requires a license, the worker must hold such a license as well. At the end of the renewal period, the worker must cease work and spend at least one year outside the U.S. before being eligible for a new H-1B visa. H-1B visas are sometimes called *high-tech visas,* because they have enabled many computer programmers and other high-tech workers to come here.

Obtaining an H-1B visa involves several steps, but they can usually be accomplished in a matter of several months or less. The employer (not the foreigner seeking to come here) is responsible for initiating the process and paying associated costs and fees. Employers can be fined for requiring reimbursement from the foreign worker.

To initiate the process, the employer determines the *prevailing wage* for the position to be filled from its state employment security agency or other appropriate source. (SESAs are listed in Appendix A.) The employer then files a *Labor Conditions Application* (LCA), Form ETA-9035CP, with the regional office of the Department of Labor. The employer must attest that:

- for the position being filled, the employer will pay at least the higher of the prevailing wage or actual wages being paid to its comparable U.S. employees;
- the proposed employment will not adversely affect working conditions of workers similarly employed;
- there is no strike in progress involving the job to be filled; and,
- the employer posted a notice of filing the LCA in conspicuous locations at its workplace.

(LCA and other Department of Labor forms are available online at **www.dol.gov/libraryforms.**)

When the LCA has been approved, the employer then files a petition with the United States Citizenship and Immigration Services (USCIS) of the Department of Homeland Security, requesting issuance of an H-1B visa. If the petition is approved, the visa itself is issued to the alien by the appropriate U.S. consulate.

In addition to paying at least the prevailing wage to the foreign worker under an H-1B visa, the employer must also offer the same range of benefits as is available to its comparable U.S. employees. Even if the worker becomes *unproductive* (benched) for some reason, he or she must still be paid. The employer must also pay for the worker's return trip home after his or her visa has expired.

H-1B visas are issued for employment by a specific employer only. If a foreign worker wants to change jobs once here, the new prospective employer must apply for a new visa. The foreign worker is not eligible for employment by the new employer until the visa is issued.

H-2B Visas

H-2B visas are somewhat similar to H-1B visas, except that they apply to a far larger pool of prospective workers—the unskilled and those whose skills fall below the professional level covered in the H-1B category. For that reason, the employer must satisfy the Secretary of Labor that it has been unable to find a sufficient number of U.S. workers who are able, willing, and qualified to fill the positions for which it seeks to import foreign workers.

H-2B visas are generally issued for one year and are renewable in one-year increments, for a total of three years.

TN Visas Under NAFTA

In addition to opening the United States' northern and southern borders to trade, the *North American Free Trade Agreement* (NAFTA) makes its easy for Canadians and Mexicans to come to the U.S. to engage in business at a professional level. A *professional* for NAFTA purposes is similar to an H-1B specialty worker—basically, a person whose job requires at least a bachelor's degree. (More information about TN visas, including a list of professionals who qualify, is available from the State Department's website at **http://travel.state.gov.**)

The procedure for Canadian nationals is simple. An employer desiring to hire a Canadian national writes a letter to the foreign worker, describing the job, agreeing to employ him or her, setting out the terms of the arrangement (salary, etc.), and the dates the employment is to begin and end. The foreign worker then appears at the Canadian border and makes application for a visa. Assuming the foreign worker can provide documentation sufficient to satisfy the immigration officer as to his or her eligibility, a one-year TN visa (which can be extended) is normally issued on the spot. The documentation should include the employment offer letter, evidence of the foreign worker's profession, and evidence that the foreign worker holds the appropriate credentials (degree, license, etc.) to engage in the work for which he or she is being hired.

For Mexican nationals, NAFTA imposes temporary quotas, and the implementing regulations prescribe a procedure that is somewhat more cumbersome than for Canadians, but still cheaper and faster than the H-1B process.

Entry under a TN visa may be denied if the Secretary of Labor certifies that entry may adversely affect the settlement of any labor dispute or the employment of any person who is involved in such dispute. In other words, an employer cannot import Canadian or Mexican workers as strike breakers.

Relatives

There is, of course, no law against *nepotism*—hiring relatives of existing employees. However, many companies have rules against doing so, particularly when the relatives will be working closely together or in a supervisor-subordinate relationship. These companies feel that the tangles and crosscurrents of family relationships add an unnecessary complication to the working environment. Further, risks of favoritism—real or apparent—could have a negative effect on the morale of other employees. Finally, having several family members on board could cause the company to suffer a double loss of productivity at vacation time or in the event of a family emergency.

On the other hand, family businesses are just that—businesses owned and operated by multiple family members, often over several generations. For example, in a restaurant or retail business in which many transactions are in cash, hiring a relative may the best way to ensure honesty and trustworthiness.

Whether or not you choose to allow nepotism, it is important to establish a policy in advance and abide by it consistently.

Former Employees

Most employment applications ask whether the candidate has ever worked for the company in the past, and if so, when and under whose supervision. If the candidate answers yes, the company is then alerted to check the candidate's personnel file and can review the reason for the prior separation. If the candidate left in good standing on a voluntary basis, say to complete a degree or for family or personal reasons, then the candidate should be eligible for rehire. The candidate's prior experience with the company, coupled with a satisfactory work history in his or her previous job, may well place him or her at a competitive advantage over other candidates whose skills and work ethic are unknown.

On the other hand, if the personnel file indicates that the candidate was terminated for cause or is otherwise ineligible for rehire, then the candidate will probably be rejected automatically. Such a policy generally makes good business sense.

> **Example**
>
> When an employee of a high-tech manufacturing company reported for work one day, he appeared to be under the influence of drugs or alcohol. A company-administered drug test proved positive for cocaine, so the employee was fired. Two years later, the employee applied for reemployment, claiming that he had recovered from his abuse problem. The company turned him down based on a note in his personnel file that he was not eligible for rehire. (The note did not indicate the specific reason for ineligibility.) The employee argued that his rejection amounted to discrimination under the *Americans with Disabilities Act* (ADA), but the U.S. Supreme Court ruled that the company's neutral no-rehire policy was a legitimate basis for rejecting the application. (The Supreme Court left open, however, the question whether the company's policy might amount to *disparate impact* discrimination. See Chapter 3.)
>
> *Raytheon Co. v. Hernandez, 124 S. Ct. 513 (2003)*

A candidate's status as a former employee, however, does not automatically eliminate all risk of discrimination.

> **Example**
>
> A truck driver for a magazine and newspaper distribution company in Chicago was laid off in a *reduction-in-force* (RIF) action by the company. His work for the company had always been satisfactory. At the time of the RIF, the driver was 51 years of age. He told the company that should any jobs become available, he would like to be rehired. A few months later, the company's business improved and it hired four new drivers, ages 30, 31, 32, and 35. The driver filed a grievance with his union, but when the company explained that it was not recalling any of the drivers that had been laid off, the union declined to pursue the grievance.
>
> *(continued)*

Later, after the driver had brought suit for age discrimination, the company offered another explanation to the effect that it only hired persons specifically referred by the union. Since there was evidence contradicting these explanations, a federal appeals court allowed the driver's age discrimination suit to go forward.

Zaccagnini v. Chas. Levy Circulating Co., 338 F.3d 672 (7th Cir. 2003)

Volunteers

In a tight labor market, students—particularly ones pursuing professional careers—may offer to work for free in order to gain experience in their fields and beef up their résumés. With very limited exceptions, however, volunteers are not a source of labor, primarily because of the *Fair Labor Standards Act* (FLSA). Since the student is performing work for which the employer normally has to pay, and the arrangement directly benefits the employer, FLSA's minimum wage and overtime requirements apply.

Example
A California nonprofit religious foundation operated various commercial businesses, including service stations, grocery outlets, hog farms, construction companies, a record-keeping company, a motel, and companies engaged in the production and distribution of candy. These businesses were staffed by so-called associates, most of whom were drug addicts, derelicts, and criminals before their conversion and rehabilitation by the foundation. The foundation provided its associates with food, shelter, clothing, and other benefits, but it did not pay them any cash wages. The associates stated that they considered themselves volunteers and considered their work part of the foundation's ministry.

(continued)

> The Department of Labor sued the foundation for violations of the FLSA, and the case eventually reached the Supreme Court. The Court pointed out that the FLSA contains no exception for religious organizations that are engaged in commercial activities. And the economic reality was that these associates were employees who were covered by the FLSA.
>
> *Alamo Foundation v. Secretary of Labor, 471 U.S. 290 (1985)*

Competitor's Employees

When you hire an employee who has previously worked for the competition or for a company in a related or similar field, you need to be concerned about possible liability under a legal doctrine known as *tortious interference with contract*. For example, you could be sued if you know that your new employee is bound by a noncompete agreement or a confidentiality agreement and you encourage the employee to breach the agreement for your benefit. Ignorance of the noncompete agreement is not likely to provide an excuse. One of the first things the former employer will do is write you a *cease and desist letter*, placing you on notice of the agreement and demanding that you respect its provisions.

Because the validity of a noncompete agreement depends on the unique circumstances of each case, it is not always easy to tell in advance whether a judge will enforce a particular agreement as written, will enforce it with modifications, or will reject it entirely as unenforceable. One thing an employer does know, however, is that litigation over a noncompete or confidentiality agreement will be costly, time-consuming, and disruptive.

When hiring a new employee, follow these guidelines to reduce the risk of suit by the employee's former employer.

- ◆ Insist on a clean break. Require your new employee to resign completely from his or her old job and cease all work for the former employer before starting the new job with you.

- Insist on reviewing any documents or files your new employee brings with him or her (or have a third party do it for you) for possible trade secrets or confidential information. Return any improperly removed materials without studying or copying them.
- Ask candidates for employment whether they are covered by noncompete or similar agreements or by any court orders or injunctions relating to employment. If they say no, get them to certify that to you in writing as part of the application process. If they say yes, get a copy of the agreement or order.
- If a candidate is covered by a noncompete or confidentiality agreement, review it carefully and have it reviewed by your attorney.
- If you decide to hire an employee who is covered by a noncompete agreement, make sure you can assign him or her work that does not violate the agreement and that you can separate him or her from any involvement—even casual lunch-time involvement—with your existing employees who are engaged in competing work.

An employer who engages in *predatory hiring* by targeting a competitor's employees—not because they are actually needed, but in order to harm the competitor's business—faces the added risk of a possible antitrust law violation. To avoid antitrust liability, the employer should be able to demonstrate a genuine business need for the employees and show that it sought qualified employees from a range of sources.

Other Restrictions

A number of federal regulatory agencies have authority to bar employment of certain individuals by the companies they regulate, typically based on prior criminal convictions. These include:

- publicly traded companies subject to Securities and Exchange Commission regulation;
- financial institutions (banks, brokerage houses, etc.) that operate under authority of the Comptroller of the Currency, the National Association of Securities Dealers, or other regulatory agencies;
- unions; and,
- government contractors.

If you are in one of these regulated industries, you need to be sure that your candidate is not barred from employment in the industry.

Your pool of potential candidates will also not include persons who do not meet the minimum requirements for the job. Various trades (such as plumbers and electricians) and professions (such as accountants and veterinarians) require state licenses. Candidates who do not have licenses and who are not in the process of obtaining them are simply unavailable.

3

Discrimination

Employment discrimination law is a complex, overlapping mix of federal, state, and local rules that prohibits employers from taking adverse employment-related actions against employees or candidates for employment based on a long list of prohibited criteria. An action is *employment-related* if it relates to *hiring, firing, compensation, or other terms, conditions, or privileges of employment.*

Adverse Action

In general, virtually any significant employment-related decision an employer makes exposes the employer to liability if it is motivated wholly or partly by discriminatory intent. However, some actions by an employer, although seemingly adverse, might be so trivial as not to amount to discrimination. A slight change in duties or a less-than-glowing evaluation without other adverse consequences might fall in this category—even if done for discriminatory reasons.

Example

An African-American electrical engineer, specializing in urban transportation systems, worked for a management consulting company. Initially, he was assigned as project manager to oversee engineering services for a subway system that was a client of the management company. However, when friction occurred between the engineer and the

(continued)

subway system contracting officer, the engineer was reassigned to another professional position and replaced by a white engineer. In his new position, the engineer received a raise and a bonus. He also received an evaluation of *highly effective,* which was one step below the *excellent* evaluation he had received the prior year. The engineer claimed race discrimination, but a federal appeals court denied his claim, saying that no adverse employment action had been taken against him. It did not matter, said the court, that the new position was less appealing to the engineer or that it might involve some additional stress not present in the old position.

James v. Booz-Allen & Hamilton, Inc. 368 F.3d 371 (4th Cir. 2004)

Disparate Treatment and Disparate Impact

The discrimination laws prohibit employers from intentionally treating one employee or group of employees differently from another employee or group based on race, religion, gender, or any of the other criteria discussed in the next chapter. This type of discrimination is sometimes known as *disparate treatment discrimination.*

Employer policies that seem nondiscriminatory on their face but have an unintended, adverse impact on certain groups can also violate discrimination laws. Examples of policies that could constitute *disparate impact discrimination,* depending upon the circumstances, include:

- ◆ a security guard company's minimum height and weight requirement that effectively excludes almost all women candidates—but almost no men candidates;
- ◆ a requirement that unskilled laborers take a written test of English, which recent immigrants are often unable to pass simply because their primary language is not English; or,

◆ a blanket policy against hiring any candidate who has a criminal record or whose wages have previously been garnished, which may tend to exclude certain minorities.

Employers are certainly free to adopt *bona fide occupational qualifications* and reject candidates who fail to meet those qualifications. But the qualifications must be based on the employer's legitimate business needs and not be just arbitrary tools that have the effect, whether intentionally or not, of discriminating.

Covered Employers

Most, but not all, federal discrimination statutes contain *threshold* requirements that make the statutes inapplicable to employers who have fewer than the specified number of employees. *Title VII*, for example, defines *employer* as a person or organization *engaged in an industry affecting commerce who has fifteen or more employees for each working day in each of twenty or more calendar weeks in the current or preceding calendar year.*

Thresholds for the principal federal discrimination laws are as follows.

◆ *Title VII of the Civil Rights Act of 1964—15 or more employees.* *Title VII* prohibits discrimination on the basis of race, color, religion, sex (including pregnancy, childbirth, and related conditions), or national origin.

◆ *Americans with Disabilities Act—15 or more employees.* The ADA prohibits discrimination against persons with disabilities and requires reasonable accommodation of persons with disabilities.

◆ *Age Discrimination in Employment Act—20 or more employees.* The ADEA prohibits discrimination against persons 40-years of-age or older on the basis of age.

◆ *Immigration Reform and Control Act—4 or more employees.* The IRCA prohibits discrimination on the basis of citizenship status or national origin. (The provisions of the IRCA prohibiting the hiring of undocumented aliens apply to *all* employers.)

Examples of federal discrimination statutes that *do not* contain threshold requirements and that apply to all employers include the following.

◆ *Equal Pay Act.* The EPA prohibits employers from paying males and females at different rates for the same work.

◆ *Section 1981.* Title 42 of the United States Code Section 1981, passed following the Civil War, guarantees to all citizens the same rights enjoyed by white citizens to make and enforce contracts.

In addition, most states and many local governments have their own discrimination laws, often with thresholds lower than their federal counterparts. So even though an employer is excluded from coverage under federal law, the employer might still be subject to the laws of the state or county in which it does business.

Counting Employees

Counting employees to determine whether these thresholds are met is not as straightforward as it may seem. One counting question involves how to deal with individuals who are carried on the employer's books as employees, but who are not physically at work for a full twenty weeks. In a 1997 Supreme Court case under *Title VII* known as *Walters v. Metropolitan Educational Enterprises*, the employer had between fifteen and seventeen employees on its payroll for at least twenty weeks, but during eleven of those weeks, it was not actually compensating fifteen or more employees.

The difference resulted from the fact that two of its employees were part-time who worked fewer than five days per week.

The Court ruled that the employer was subject to *Title VII*, adopting what has become known as the *payroll method* for counting employees. Under that method, if an employee appears on the employer's payroll records, he or she is counted whether or not he or she is actually being compensated on a particular day.

Employees and Independent Contractors

Another question involves the distinction between employees and independent contractors. In the case of *Nationwide Mutual Insurance Co. v. Darden*, which arose under the *Employee Retirement Income Security Act*, the Supreme Court concluded that Congress intended to incorporate common-law principles in determining whether a worker was an employee or an independent contractor. In general, a worker is considered an employee under the common law if the employer has the right to control the manner and means by which the worker performs his or her duties.

Owner-Employees

Yet another question involves shareholder-directors of professional corporations, such as doctors, lawyers, etc. While they may be classified as employees for federal tax and pension plan purposes, they also own and run the professional corporation. In a Supreme Court case called *Clackamas Gastroenterology Associates v. Wells*, the bookkeeper at an Oregon medical clinic sued the clinic for discrimination. The bookkeeper argued that the clinic met the fifteen-employee threshold so long as four of its physician-shareholders were counted. The bookkeeper pointed out, for example, that the physician-shareholders had employment contracts, they were salaried, and they were treated as employees for tax purposes. The clinic claimed otherwise—that the physician-shareholders were really more like partners in a partnership and should therefore not be counted.

The Supreme Court, relying on its earlier *Darden* decision, ruled that *common-law principles* should apply and listed the following six factors to be considered in determining whether a shareholder-director of a professional corporation is an employee for discrimination purposes:

1. whether the organization can hire or fire the individual or set the rules and regulations of the individual's work (tends to make the individual an employee;

2. whether—and, if so, to what extent—the organization supervises the individual's work (tends to make the individual an employee);

3. whether the individual reports to someone higher in the organization (tends to make the individual an employee);

4. whether—and, if so, to what extent—the individual is able to influence the organization (tends to make the individual a non-employee owner);

5. whether the parties intended that the individual be an employee, as expressed in written contracts; and,

6. whether the individual shares in the profits, losses, and liabilities of the organization (tends to make the individual a non-employee owner).

Affiliated Companies

Under the *single employer doctrine*, when two companies are highly integrated with respect to ownership and management, they will be considered one company for employee-counting purposes. So even though neither company alone has the requisite number of employees to be covered by a particular federal discrimination law, if the number of employees in the aggregate meets the threshold requirement, both companies will be subject to the law.

In determining whether the single employer doctrine should apply, the courts look to the degree to which companies have interrelated operations, common management, centralized control of labor relations, and common ownership.

Foreign Employment

Activities by employers outside the U.S. could certainly affect commerce within the U.S. However, the Supreme Court has held that *Title VII* does not have extraterritorial application, so that U.S. citizens employed abroad—even U.S. citizens employed by U.S. employers—have no protection under U.S. discrimination laws. *Title VII* itself exempts aliens employed outside the U.S. and it permits employers operating in a foreign country to comply with that country's law, even if compliance amounts to a violation of *Title VII*.

In general, foreign employers doing business in the U.S. must comply with U.S. discrimination laws as a privilege of doing business here, whether they employ U.S. citizens or their own foreign nationals. But there is an exception based on treaties the U.S. has with many foreign countries. *Friendship, Commerce, and Navigation* (FCN) *treaties* permit foreign companies doing business in the U.S. to choose whatever high-level, essential personnel they wish. These treaty provisions have been held to permit foreign companies to discriminate in favor of their own nationals, even though doing so would otherwise constitute race or national origin discrimination.

Another exception is based on the *Foreign Sovereign Immunities Act* (FSIA). Under the FSIA, *foreign states* are immune from the jurisdiction of courts in the U.S., so long as they are engaged in governmental-type activities (as opposed to commercial activities).

Example

Saudi Arabia hired a U.S. security firm to work with the Saudis' own military in providing protection for members of the Saudi royal family living in the U.S. A female employee of the security firm requested assignment to a command post staffed by members of the Saudi military. The assignment would have required her to spend long periods working with her Saudi male counterparts. The Saudi military objected on the basis that working in close proximity with females would be unacceptable under Islamic law. The employee was denied the assignment, even though she was fully qualified for the position. A federal appeals court ruled that not only were the Saudis immune under the FSIA, but the security firm, even though it was a U.S. company, enjoyed *derivative immunity* when following the instructions of the foreign sovereign.

Butters v. Vance Int'l, Inc., 225 F.3d 462 (4th Cir. 2000)

4

Specific Types of Discrimination

With few exceptions, most employers who meet the minimum statutory thresholds are prohibited by federal law from considering certain criteria when taking an employment-related action or making a decision regarding candidates for employment. These criteria include:

- race;
- color;
- religion;
- sex;
- pregnancy, childbirth, and related conditions;
- national origin and ancestry;
- age;
- disability;
- citizenship status;
- military and veteran status; and,
- union membership.

The Equal Employment Opportunity Commission's website at **www.eeoc.gov** has guidelines on various forms of discrimination. States and local jurisdictions often add additional prohibited criteria to the list, such as:

- marital or family status;
- sexual orientation;

- appearance;
- family responsibilities; and,
- genetics.

Many of the terms, such as race, color, and national origin, are easily understood in the employment context. Other criteria, however, involve special considerations.

Religion

Title VII makes it illegal for an employer to discriminate against an employee on the basis of his or her religion. *Religion* includes all aspects of religious observance, practice, and belief. This means that an employer cannot refuse to hire a candidate because he or she is a member of a particular religious sect, just as the employer similarly cannot refuse to hire a candidate on the basis of his or her race or gender.

Employers also have a duty to *reasonably accommodate* their employees' religious observances or practices, unless doing so would impose an *undue hardship* on the conduct of the employer's business. In this respect, religious discrimination is similar to discrimination under the *Americans with Disabilities Act* (ADA), under which employers have an affirmative duty to reasonably accommodate their employees' disabilities. As with the ADA, the burden is on the employee to ask for a reasonable religious accommodation.

> ### Example
> A licensed pharmacist applied for a position at a drug store. During the interview, he stated that selling birth control devices was contrary to his religious beliefs and he asked that the employer not require him to do so. The employer decided that no accommodation was possible and it refused to consider the pharmacist's application. The employer was guilty of religious
>
> *(continued)*

> discrimination because it made no effort at accommodation and because
> its claim of undue hardship was merely speculative.
>
> *Hellinger v. Eckerd Corp., 67 F. Supp. 2d 1359 (S.D.Fla. 1999)*

Special rules apply to religious organizations. The First Amendment to the U.S. Constitution says that *Congress shall make no law respecting the establishment of religion, or prohibiting the free exercise thereof.* Based on the First Amendment, the courts have developed the so-called *ministerial exception* to *Title VII*, under which religious organizations *may* discriminate in connection with the selection and employment of their own clergy. Even for non-clergy, religious organizations may discriminate against employees on *religious* grounds.

The ministerial exception has its limits, however, as illustrated by a recent case that arose in Washington State.

Example

An ordained female minister was hired as associate pastor for a local Presbyterian Church. After taking the position, she was allegedly subject to harassment by her supervising pastor. When she complained to higher church authorities, she was suspended without pay and then fired. Church authorities also prohibited her from circulating her résumé to other churches, effectively barring her from employment in any Presbyterian church in the U.S. She then sued for sex discrimination and retaliation, but the Church defended on First Amendment grounds, claiming that court involvement in its employment decision would amount to unconstitutional interference with religion.

The trial court agreed with the Church and dismissed the suit, but a federal appeals court reversed the decision. The appellate court recognized that a religious organization's decision to employ or terminate a

(continued)

> minister is at the heart of its religious mission. Therefore, the minister could not base her claims on the allegation that she was suspended and then fired in retaliation for her harassment complaint. However, she *could* sue the Church for emotional damages caused by the alleged harassment itself. The appellate court reached its conclusion because the factual issues involved in that claim—whether the minister was in fact harassed, and whether the Church responded reasonably to stop the harassment after she complained—do not intrude on religious doctrine.
>
> *McDowell v. Calvin Presbyterian Church, 375 F.3d 951 (9th Cir. 2004)*

Sex

Except in very limited circumstances, an employer cannot prefer male candidates over female candidates (or vice versa) based on the candidates' gender.

> ### Example
>
> Lead, a component in certain types of batteries, poses substantial health risks, including risks to fetuses carried by pregnant women who are exposed to the substance. When a battery manufacturer discovered high lead levels in the blood of a number of its pregnant employees, the company adopted a policy barring all women of child-bearing age from jobs involving exposure to lead, unless they could document that they were incapable of having children. The Supreme Court held that the policy amounted to sex discrimination despite the company's benign motives. The Court said that the policy could not be justified as a *bona fide occupational qualification* (BFOQ), since there was no evidence that pregnant women were less able than others to manufacture batteries.
>
> *(continued)*

> The Court concluded that the question of fetal safety should be for the mother, not the company to decide. It dismissed as only a remote possibility the company's fear of suit by children with birth defects attributed to fetal lead exposure.
>
> *United Auto Workers v. Johnson Controls, Inc., 499 U.S. 187 (1991)*

Pregnancy, Childbirth, and Related Conditions

In 1978 Congress passed the *Pregnancy Discrimination Act* (PDA), which amended *Title VII* to define discrimination because of sex as including discrimination because of or on account of pregnancy, childbirth, or related medical conditions. In other words, discrimination because of pregnancy, childbirth, or a related medical condition is sex discrimination. Therefore, an employer cannot refuse to hire a pregnant woman because of her pregnancy or a woman of child-bearing age because of the possibility she may become pregnant.

Age

The expressed purpose of the *Age Discrimination in Employment Act* (ADEA) is to promote employment of older persons based on their ability rather than their age. The ADEA accomplishes this purpose by prohibiting age-based discrimination against employees and job candidates 40 years-of-age or older. An age-based decision affecting a person under age 40 does not violate the ADEA. (Many states and local jurisdictions have their own age discrimination laws that apply to all employees, not just those 40 years-of-age or older.)

As with *Title VII*, there is an exception in the ADEA for a *bona fide occupational qualification* (BFOQ). However, the exception has been very narrowly applied by the courts.

> ## Example
>
> An airline had a rule that its flight engineers must retire at age 60, on the theory that many persons over that age have limitations that preclude safe operation of an aircraft. The airline argued that it would be impractical, if not impossible, to examine all flight engineers and identify those with limitations. A jury found the rule illegal under the ADEA and awarded damages. The Supreme Court let the jury verdict stand, saying that it was not enough for the airline to have a rational basis for its policy. Instead, the airline had to prove that its policy was reasonably necessary to the normal operation or essence of the particular business.
>
> *Western Air Lines, Inc. v. Criswell, 472 U.S. 400 (1985)*

When it comes to reverse discrimination, the ADEA is different from other forms of discrimination. Under *Title VII*, for example, it is just as illegal to favor minorities and women as it is to favor whites and males. In other words, *Title VII* is color blind and gender neutral. Instead of protecting *specific groups*, it targets *prohibited criteria* (race, gender, etc.).

In contrast, the ADEA does protect a specific group—workers 40 years-of-age or older. So if, for example, a covered employer fires a 55-year-old and replaces him or her with someone who is only age 30, and the employer does so on the basis of age, then the employer has violated the ADEA. At the same time, firing a 30-year-old and replacing him or her with someone who is age 55 on the basis of age is not illegal under the ADEA. But what if both the individuals involved are at least age 40 and in the protected group? Is favoring a 45-year-old over someone who is age 60 illegal? How about favoring the 60-year-old over a worker age 45?

In 1996, the Supreme Court answered the second question, ruling that when an older worker is replaced by someone younger because of age, the employer has violated the ADEA. It does not matter, said the Court, that the younger worker is also in the 40-and-older protected class, since a claim of age discrimination can be based just on a significant age difference.

In February 2004, the Court answered the third question, ruling that an employer's practice that favors older workers is permitted under the ADEA, even though it discriminates against younger workers who are in the age 40 and over protected class. The case involved a company health insurance plan that extended certain benefits to employees 50 years-of-age and older, but denied those benefits to younger employees. The Court said that even though the plan discriminated against workers between the ages of 40 and 49 based on age, the the ADEA is aimed at protecting older workers, not younger ones. In other words, the ADEA does not *look both ways*.

Disability

The *Americans with Disabilities Act* (ADA) prohibits discrimination against a *qualified individual with a disability* with respect to application procedures, hiring, promotion, discharge, compensation, training, and other terms, conditions, and privileges of employment. A *qualified individual* is a person who, with or without *reasonable accommodation*, can perform the essential functions of the job he or she is applying for.

In short, an employer cannot reject a candidate because the candidate has a disability if, despite the disability, the candidate can perform the essential functions of the job. Further, if the candidate cannot perform the essential functions of the job but *could do so with reasonable accommodation*, then the employer must provide that accommodation—unless it would impose an *undue hardship*.

As used in the ADA, *disability* means a physical or mental impairment that substantially limits one or more major life activities. The Equal Employment Opportunity Commission, which is charged with enforcing the employment provisions of the ADA, defines *major life activity* to include hearing, seeing, speaking, breathing, performing manual tasks, walking, caring for oneself, learning, and working.

Virtually any condition that can be diagnosed by a physician or psychotherapist (other than a temporary condition) is an impairment within the meaning of the ADA. If the impairment does not substantially limit one or more major life activities, however, it is not a disability for ADA purposes. By contrast, the list of exclusions from ADA coverage is short. It includes:

- homosexuality and bisexuality (because they are not considered impairments);
- transvestism, transsexualism, pedophilia, exhibitionism, voyeurism, gender identity disorders not resulting from physical impairment, or other sexual behavior disorders;
- compulsive gambling;
- kleptomania;
- pyromania; and,
- psychoactive substance abuse disorders resulting from current illegal use of drugs.

It is important to note that the existence of even a significant impairment does not necessarily render a person disabled. An individualized, case-by-case inquiry is required to determine whether a particular employee is in fact substantially limited in one or more major life activities.

Example
Twin sisters applied to an airline for employment as commercial pilots. The airline rejected them because they each suffered from severe visual myopia, although with glasses they functioned identically with other individuals who did not have myopia. The Supreme Court ruled that mitigating measures should be taken into consideration when judging

(continued)

whether the candidates were disabled. It said the ADA requires that a person be presently—not potentially or hypothetically—substantially limited in order to demonstrate a disability. A disability exists only when an impairment substantially limits a major life activity, not when it might or could or would be substantially limiting if mitigating measures were not taken. While persons with conditions like severe myopia may have an impairment, once the impairment is corrected, they are not substantially limited in any major life activity, as required by the ADA. Since the sisters here were not disabled, they had no ADA protection.

Sutton v. United Airlines, Inc., 523 U.S. 471 (1999)

Addiction to drugs or alcohol is an impairment that may trigger ADA coverage, depending on each particular individual's circumstances. However, employers *may* discriminate against current, illegal drug users.

The ADA has special rules for medical examinations. Prior to actually offering employment, an employer may *never* require a candidate to undergo a medical exam. While testing for illegal drugs is not considered a medical exam and is permitted prior to making a job offer, just about every other form of pre-offer medical test—including AIDS testing and genetic testing—is illegal.

When the employer actually *offers* employment, it may condition the offer on the results of a medical exam if:

- all entering employees in the job category are subject to examination;
- the exam requirement can be shown to be job-related and consistent with business necessity;
- the resulting medical information is separately maintained and treated as confidential; and,
- the results are not used to discriminate against persons with disabilities.

Closely related to medical examinations are disability-related inquiries. In general, an employer may not ask a candidate about a disability and may not ask questions designed to elicit information about a disability. An employer may ask whether a candidate can perform job functions, whether an employee has been drinking, and about current illegal drug use. Once a candidate discloses information about a disability and requests an accommodation, however, the employer is then *required* to make disability-related inquiries.

If a candidate informs the employer of his or her disability and requests the employer to accommodate, the employer must do so unless the accommodation is *unreasonable* or would impose an *undue hardship*—that is, the accommodation would be significantly difficult or expensive. It is often difficult to know whether a requested accommodation is reasonable or is an undue hardship. The ADA gives some examples of what is reasonable. For one, the employer's facilities must be readily accessible and usable. Wheelchair ramps may have to be installed and doorways and restroom facilities may need to be enlarged. Other examples might include:

- restructuring jobs;
- modifying work schedules;
- relaxing workplace rules;
- making reassignments to vacant positions; and,
- modifying or replacing existing equipment.

What employers need to remember is that when a disabled candidate requests an accommodation, the employer must engage in a good faith interactive process with the candidate to identify accommodations that might enable him or her to perform the essential functions of the job. It could be that no accommodation will actually work, or that while a particular accommodation might work, it is unreasonable or would impose an undue hardship. Should that be the case, the employer is free to reject the candidate. But if the employer fails to engage in an interactive process, the employer will almost certainly lose any ADA suit that follows.

Military and Veteran Status

Federal law prohibits employers from discriminating against candidates on account of their military service. Persons who are members of the uniformed services, who have applied to become members, or who have obligations to one of the uniformed services are protected against discrimination in hiring, retention, reemployment, promotion, or the granting of any employment benefit.

Union Membership

The *National Labor Relations Act* (NLRA) makes it an unfair labor practice for an employer to discriminate with regards to hiring or tenure of employment or any term or condition of employment to encourage or discourage membership in any labor organization. Simply stated, an employer cannot reject a candidate because the candidate is a union member or organizer, or because the candidate has previously engaged or organizational efforts or other union activity.

Sexual Orientation

Most courts that have considered the question have concluded that *Title VII's* prohibition against discrimination because of sex does not cover sexual orientation discrimination. However, many state and local laws do prohibit this type of discrimination. Even when not prohibited at the state or local level, rejection of a candidate based on his or her sexual preferences could amount to violations of other laws, such as those prohibiting discrimination based on family status, marital status, appearance, etc.

Genetics

It is understandable that employers would want to know which of their candidates for employment are at risk for genetically linked diseases. While there are no federal laws specifically prohibiting an employer from obtaining genetic information and using it to screen candidates, the practice could indirectly run afoul of other federal laws. It certainly does run afoul of state and local laws that specifically prohibit discrimination on the basis of genetics. Some of the federal laws that could make discrimination on the basis of genetics illegal include the following.

- The ADA prohibits all *pre-employment* medical examinations (except drug testing). A test for genetic markers undoubtedly falls within this prohibition and is therefore illegal.

- The ADA prohibits discrimination against persons who are *regarded as* disabled. The EEOC takes the view that this provision prohibits discrimination based on genetics, but that view has not been tested in the courts as of this writing.

- To the extent genetic conditions are more prevalent in certain races or in persons of certain ancestries (sickle cell anemia, for example), genetic screening could amount to race or national origin discrimination.

- The *Health Insurance Portability and Accountability Act* (HIPAA) prohibits group health insurance plans from establishing eligibility rules based on *health status-related factors*, which include genetic information. Also under HIPAA, genetic information cannot be used to conclude that a person has a preexisting condition. The conclusion can only be based on a diagnosis of the condition itself.

- U.S. Department of Health and Human Services regulations under HIPAA prohibit group health plans from disclosing protected health information to plan sponsors, except to enable plan sponsors to carry out plan administration functions that the plan sponsor performs.

Reverse Discrimination

Discrimination laws were originally intended to eliminate biases against minorities and women, who historically have been the victims of workplace prejudice. But the laws go well beyond those specific groups. It is just as illegal, for example, for an employer to favor a black candidate over a white candidate because of race, or to pay women higher salaries than men based on their gender. This type of discrimination is sometimes known as *reverse discrimination.* In fact, most discrimination laws do not protect specific groups at all. Instead, they prohibit employers from using certain *criteria,* such as race, religion, etc., in making employment decisions, regardless of who might be favored or disfavored.

Recent Supreme Court developments may have muddied the legal waters a bit concerning reverse discrimination. In June 2003, the Court ruled that the University of Michigan law school could consider race as a plus factor in evaluating applicants to the law school, because the school had a legitimate interest in assembling a diverse student body. (At the same time, the Court invalidated a procedure that awarded bonus points to racial minorities who were applying to the university's undergraduate school.)

Since employers also have an interest in assembling a diverse workplace, it is possible that some limited form of reverse discrimination by employers is permissible. Future court decisions will likely address this issue.

Testers and Salts

A *tester* is as an individual who, without the intent of accepting an offer of employment, poses as a job candidate in order to gather evidence of discriminatory hiring practices. For example, when an employer is suspected of race discrimination, pairs of white and black individuals with similar résumés apply for an opening. If the black candidates are consistently told that their references will have to be checked, but the white candidates are offered jobs on the spot, it is reasonable to conclude that the employer practices race discrimination.

Since a tester is not really looking for work, it could be argued that a refusal to hire a tester, no matter what the motivation, does not amount to discrimination. Stated in legal terms, a tester does not have *standing* to complain because he or she has not really been hurt by the employer's otherwise unlawful action.

The Equal Employment Opportunity Commission (EEOC) and a few courts take the view that testers do have standing and can sue for discrimination even if they would have turned down an offer of employment. Other courts have reached the opposite conclusion.

The U.S. Supreme Court ruled a number of years ago that testers may bring suit for violations of the *Fair Housing Act*. The Court has not, however, decided the issue as it relates to employment discrimination.

In an effort to unionize a nonunion shop, a union may attempt to *salt* the shop by sending union organizers as candidates for job openings. Unlike a tester, a salt is actually seeking employment, but his or her real purpose is to organize the shop once hired. When an employer refuses to hire, or even consider, such candidates and the employer is motivated, at least in part, by *antiunion animus*, the employer commits an unfair labor practice.

5

Procedures and Remedies for Discrimination

This section outlines—in general terms—the course of a typical employment discrimination charge and the remedies that are potentially available to victims of discrimination. This chapter is *not* intended as a do-it-yourself guide to defending a charge of discrimination. When faced with a charge, employers should consult experienced employment counsel. (For more information about procedures and remedies, go to the EEOC's website at **www.eeoc.gov.**)

Filing a Charge

An unsuccessful candidate for employment who feels he or she has been rejected for discriminatory reasons may notify the employer involved and ask for reconsideration. More likely, the candidate will go straight to a local office of the Equal Employment Opportunity Commission (EEOC) or to a state or local fair employment practices agency (FEPA) and file a formal charge of discrimination.

For most types of discrimination prohibited by federal law, filing a charge with the EEOC or a FEPA is a prerequisite to suing in court. The only exceptions are suits under the *Equal Pay Act* and Section 1981.

Often, the EEOC and a state or local FEPA will each have jurisdiction over a particular charge. When that is the case, the charge will be *dual filed*—whichever agency first receives the charge will transmit a copy to the other agency. Normally, the agency that first receives the charge will take the lead in handling the charge. However, *work-sharing agreements* between the EEOC and the FEPA may provide otherwise.

A charge of discrimination must be filed with the EEOC within 180 days after the alleged discrimination occurred. If the charge is also covered under state or local discrimination laws, the 180-day time limit is extended to 300 days.

Processing a Charge

On receipt of a charge, the EEOC will first determine whether it has jurisdiction. It must decide:

- whether the type of discrimination being charged, if it in fact occurred, would violate federal law;
- whether the charging individual is an employee or candidate for employment; and,
- whether the employer has a sufficient number of employees to meet any applicable threshold.

If the EEOC has jurisdiction, it will then notify the employer of the charge and begin an investigation.

Often, the first time an employer becomes aware that it has been accused of discrimination is when the employer receives a *Notice of Charge of Discrimination* (EEOC Form 131). The Notice will normally include a copy of the charge itself and it will identify the type of discrimination being charged (race, age, disability, etc.). It is usually in the employer's best interest to cooperate with the EEOC at this juncture. (If the EEOC serves the employer with a *subpoena* for documents and records, not cooperating may not be an option.)

Typically, the EEOC will request the employer to file a *position statement* stating the employer's position with respect to the charge. The EEOC's investigation may also include a request for employer documents and records, an on-site inspection, and interviews of management-level and other employees. If the EEOC concludes that no discrimination has occurred, the EEOC will notify the parties, close its case, and issue a *right-to-sue* letter to the employee. If the EEOC concludes that discrimination *has* occurred, the parties will be informed and the EEOC will attempt to *conciliate* the matter by seeking the parties' agreement on appropriate remedies. If the conciliation is successful, that will end the matter—unless one of the parties later violates the conciliation agreement.

If conciliation is unsuccessful, the EEOC will either issue a *right-to-sue letter* to the employee or it may decide to bring suit itself against the employer. The EEOC may decide to sue as plaintiff if, for example, the case involves an important but unresolved legal principle or if a large number of employees is involved.

For most types of discrimination, an employee has ninety days after receiving a right-to-sue letter to file suit in court. If the claim involves a violation of federal discrimination laws, suit can be brought either in federal district court or in state court. If only state or local discrimination laws are involved, the victim will normally be limited to suing in state court.

Available Remedies

Once discrimination is found, a wide variety of remedies are available under federal law. These may be classified as either *victim-specific remedies* or *general remedies*. Victim-specific remedies are intended to make the victim whole by placing the victim in the position he or she would have been in if the discrimination had not taken place. *General remedies* are focused on curing faulty workplace practices.

Victim-specific remedies include:

- ◆ requiring the employer to *hire* the rejected candidate (and to provide reasonable accommodation, in cases of disability discrimination);

- awarding the victim *backpay* (the pay he or she would have received between the time of the discrimination and the date of the award);
- awarding *frontpay* (the pay the victim would have received from the time of the award to some reasonable time in the future) when hiring the rejected candidate is not feasible;
- awarding *compensatory damages* (which can include damages for emotional pain and suffering);
- awarding *punitive damages* to punish the employer; and,
- requiring the employer to pay the victim's *attorney fees*, *expert witness fees*, and *court costs*.

A party seeking compensatory or punitive damages is entitled to a jury trial. However, the amount of compensatory and punitive damages that may be awarded under federal law is subject to dollar limitations (*caps*) depending on the number of employees the employer has. The following chart shows the cap amounts based on number of employees.

Number of employees	Cap
Between 15 and 100	$50,000
Between 101 and 200	$100,000
Between 201 and 500	$200,000
More than 500	$300,000

Example

After Albert received a bachelor's degree in Bible studies, he worked as a church pastor and later in a school for the mentally retarded. He then left active ministry and took a job as a custodian at a printing company in Maine, but he remained very religious. Albert's supervisor at the printing company learned about Albert's religious views when Albert

(continued)

asked for Sundays off. Apparently having a low regard for those views, the supervisor embarked on an eight-year campaign of ridiculing Albert, his religion, his strict sobriety, and his unwillingness to womanize. The supervisor's harassment included obscene references to Christian religious figures.

Albert's complaints to Human Resources were unavailing, so Albert finally quit, which the court treated as a *constructive discharge* (the equivalent of being fired). Albert was quickly able to obtain replacement work at a supermarket, but was later fired from that job for violating a supermarket rule against eating food that had not been paid for.

In Albert's suit against the printing company for religious discrimination, a jury awarded him $1,150,000 in compensatory and punitive damages, which the court reduced to the statutory cap of $300,000. However, the court would not allow the jury to award backpay or front-pay past the date Albert was fired from his supermarket job, ruling that Albert had failed to *mitigate* his damages. In other words, Albert's own misconduct at the supermarket, not his constructive discharge by the printing company, caused his subsequent lost wages.

Johnson v. Spencer Press of Maine, Inc., 364 F.3d 368 (1st Cir. 2004)

General remedies (remedies that are not victim-specific) include:

- an injunction, which forbids the employer from discriminating in the future;
- a requirement that the employer post notices in the workplace concerning the violation and employees' rights under the law; and,
- a requirement that the employer provide training or take other measures to prevent future discrimination and submit compliance reports to the EEOC.

State and local discrimination laws provide similar remedies, but without the caps. For that reason, victims will often combine both federal and state or local claims in their suits.

6

Job Description

Once the decision to hire has been made, the employer's very next step should be to prepare or update a *job description*. An accurate and complete written description of the job to be filled is an invaluable tool for many reasons. Some of the most important reasons are the following.

- It helps identify the *skills and qualifications* the employer should be looking for in a candidate.
- It provides a *convenient reference* for recruiting.
- It assures that all potential candidates receive the *same information* about the job.
- It provides a basis for determining whether the position is *exempt* or *nonexempt* under the federal *Fair Labor Standards Act* and state wage-and-hour laws.
- It informs candidates what will be *expected of them* if hired and it demonstrates to candidates that the employer is *organized*, *businesslike*, and *professional*.
- It provides a standard against which candidates can be *compared* with each other.
- It provides a standard against which a candidate, once hired and on the job, can be *evaluated*.

- It helps employers establish *fair compensation ranges* for various jobs.
- It provides *powerful ammunition* in defending later discrimination claims by identifying essential job functions before any candidates are considered.

This last point merits emphasis. In cases of disability discrimination, for example, the ADA requires courts to consider the employer's judgment as to what functions of a job are essential. Consequently, courts generally will not second-guess the employer's judgment, as long as functions identified as essential are *job-related*, *uniformly enforced*, and *consistent with business necessity*.

On the other hand, if the employer has not prepared a job description in advance, then the employer is much more vulnerable to a claim of disability discrimination. As the following example shows, courts will likely be skeptical of an after-the-fact employer determination that a particular function is essential and that rejection of a disabled candidate was justified.

Example

The manager at a truck repair shop in Ohio was diagnosed with lung cancer and took extended leave for surgery and radiation treatment. He returned to work about a year later, but his breathing remained seriously compromised. After being back on the job only a short time, the manager was discharged because, according to his supervisor, he was not physically fit to do the work. When pressed about this statement, the supervisor mentioned the need to lift and move batteries and tires weighing 150 pounds. At the time, the manager's job was mainly supervisory, although his written job description did mention *lifting (min. 50 lbs.)*.

The manager sued under the ADA and recovered a jury verdict for $950,000. On appeal, the federal Sixth Circuit Court of Appeals

(continued)

> upheld the verdict, ruling the employer had failed to establish that *repetitive lifting* of 50-pound truck batteries and 150-pound truck tires was part of the job. In fact, according to the evidence, such lifting was relatively rare, and therefore not an essential function of the job.
>
> *U-Haul Co. of Cleveland v. Kunkle, 165 F.3d 29 (6th Cir. 1998)*

Contents of Description

A good job description should contain the following elements:

- the *title* of the position;
- a description of the *essential functions* of the position—that is, the functions that the employee *must* be able to perform;
- a description of *other functions* that, though not essential, are normally or occasionally performed by persons holding the position;
- any *skills* the employee will need and any *equipment* or *tools* the employee will be required to use;
- any *unusual aspects* of the job, such as *substantial overtime required, occasional overseas travel,* or *security clearance needed*;
- a description of where the position falls on the company's *organizational chart*—that is, the position to which the employee reports and the positions that report to the employee;
- whether the position is *exempt* or *nonexempt* under the federal *Fair Labor Standards Act* and state wage-and-hour laws; and,
- the date it was prepared or most recently updated.

Job descriptions might also state the method of compensation (salaried, hourly, commission, etc.) and the compensation range. An ending tagline such as *and other duties as assigned* is fine, so long as those other duties are not considered essential. (A sample job description for a paralegal at a law firm is located on the following page.)

Sample Job Description

PARALEGAL (Litigation Support)

Exempt/Nonexempt status: Nonexempt

Primary duties:

- Interviews witnesses and investigates factual claims and defenses
- Researches law (statutes, regulations, reported court and agency decisions, treatises, etc.) and prepares memoranda of law
- Analyzes and organizes discovery materials
- Drafts pleadings, motions, discovery requests, discovery responses, and briefs for review by attorney
- Maintains pleading and document files and litigation calendar
- Schedules depositions
- Attends and assists at depositions, hearings, and trials

Other duties:

- Files pleadings and other papers with courts and administrative agencies
- Messengers documents to and from clients and opposing attorneys
- Serves subpoenas
- Assists in maintaining law library

Special requirements/qualifications: Paralegal certificate or equivalent experience required. Person holding this position must be able to write in clear, grammatically correct English; must be proficient using word processing, spreadsheet, presentation, and time and billing computer software; and, must be proficient using electronic legal research databases.

Position reports to: Head attorney, Litigation Section

Direct reports to position: None

Compensation basis and range: Salary, $28,000–$55,000 per year

Date prepared/updated: November 2004

Minimum educational or other qualifications are sometimes included in job descriptions, such as *bachelor's degree required* or *three years' experience needed.* Unless the employer can show that such qualifications are essential, they pose a danger of being discriminatory. However, if the qualification is essential, it should be stated in the description.

Employers should also keep in mind that jobs change over time. For example, the company's products and services may evolve, duties may be eliminated or expanded, or technology changes may require new skills. A periodic review and updating of job descriptions is therefore essential.

Describing Duties

A number of companies sell commercially prepared job descriptions. A search for *job descriptions* on the Internet will return dozens of sites, some of which even provide descriptions for free. Another useful resource is the *Dictionary of Occupational Titles*, published by the U.S. Department of Labor's Employment and Training Administration. It is available from the Government Printing Office at **http://bookstore.gpo.gov**.

While these sources may be a helpful starting point, your job descriptions need to be specifically tailored to your organization. An off-the-shelf description that does not accurately describe what your employee will be doing is worse than no description at all.

A good job description requires *job analysis*—an in-depth study of the job. The analyst should interview employees who are currently performing the job, perhaps ask them to fill out a questionnaire, observe them at work, and interview other employees and supervisors who interact with the position being analyzed.

A draft description is then circulated to the incumbent and his or her supervisor for comment. At this point, the supervisor may want to suggest that the job be restructured by adding duties that the employee could be expected to perform or by eliminating duties that could be more efficiently performed by others. A final description is then submitted to management for approval.

7

Recruiting

An employer has a wide variety of recruiting methods available, such as:

- word-of-mouth;
- posting at the workplace;
- running classified ads in local or national newspapers;
- posting on the employer's own website or posting on Internet job banks;
- attending job fairs;
- contacting school placement officers; and,
- engaging employment agencies and headhunters.

The wider the net the employer casts, the greater the number of candidates that are likely to respond, assuring the employer a large field from which to choose. Casting a wide net also has the advantage of generating a *diverse field of candidates*, reducing the risk that a more narrowly focused method will be found discriminatory.

> **Example**
>
> A family-run company is in the business of making and repairing hand-held tools. It has forty-five employees, almost all of whom are white. When a sales position opened up, the company used word-of-mouth to let its existing staff know about the opening. It filled the position with a white candidate. None of the black employees applied for the position because they did not know about the opening until after it was filled. A federal court of appeals ruled that the company's failure to advertise its job openings and post notices of available positions created a presumption of intent to discriminate and it allowed a black employee's suit for discrimination to go forward.
>
> *Carmichael v. Birmingham Saw Works, 738 F.2d 1126 (11th Cir. 1984)*

The problem with casting a wide net is *résumé overload*. Commercially available software can be used to screen résumés, eliminate unqualified candidates, and rank the remaining candidates for individual review. Employers can even program the software to search for whatever key words they wish. However, unless the screening process is carefully designed so as not to be culturally or otherwise biased, the process could be discriminatory. Even requiring that résumés be submitted electronically could amount to disparate impact discrimination if certain groups of otherwise qualified candidates have limited access to the Internet.

Casting a wide net may not be practical for every job. It would make no sense to advertise a part-time custodial position with the local college placement office. Nor would it make sense to place an ad in a weekly paper of limited distribution for a programmer with experience in an obscure computer language.

Classified Ads

There was a time when newspaper help-wanted ads were explicitly discriminatory, telling readers that persons of certain races, ethnicity, or ancestry need not apply. The *Civil Rights Act of 1964* made that practice illegal. It is an unlawful employment practice to print or publish any notice or advertisement indicating any preference, limitation, specification, or discrimination based on race, color, religion, sex, or national origin. In one case, for example, an airline's help-wanted ad for *stewardesses* was held illegal because it indicated a preference for female candidates.

More subtle indications of preference could also amount to discrimination. For example, an ad for *energetic college graduate* suggests age discrimination. An ad for a *gal Friday* office assistant obviously connotes gender.

Referral Bonuses

Some companies use their existing employees as recruiters by paying them a bonus for referring candidates that are actually hired by the company. The bonus usually does not become payable until the candidate has stayed on the job for some minimum time period, such as ninety days or six months.

The advantage of this approach is that the news of an opening gets spread quickly by people who are familiar with the company and its culture, and who presumably like where they work. The disadvantage is that it tends to limit diversity.

8

Résumés and Résumé Fraud

The first contact between a candidate and a prospective employer is usually via the candidate's résumé. By providing a snapshop of the candidate's interests, education, work experience, skills, and social activities, a résumé enables the employer to determine quickly whether the candidate should be rejected *out-of-hand* or deserves further consideration.

Perhaps it is this *getting noticed* function of résumés that induces candidates to hype their credentials by exaggerating the responsibilities of prior positions, omitting jobs from which they were fired, inflating grade-point averages, and adding degrees never earned. Reports in the press say half of all résumés contain false or misleading information. Candidates have even been known to pay hackers to add their names to university databases and give prospective employers bogus phone numbers that, when called, will falsely verify credentials.

While ferreting out these lies is becoming increasingly burdensome, there are a number of steps employers can take to assure that they get an accurate picture of the candidate. These steps include:

- checking all references;
- asking each reference to furnish the name of another person who knows the candidate—and check with that person as well;

- requiring the candidate to complete a standard written employment application and checking the application against the résumé for inconsistencies;
- including in the application a certification by the candidate that the application is truthful, that all supporting items (such as transcripts and reference letters) are genuine, and that false, misleading, or incomplete statements are grounds for termination;
- having technicians participate in interviewing the candidate if the candidate claims knowledge or experience in a particular technical field;
- requiring candidates to present original documentation in support of résumé claims (degrees, certifications, drivers' licenses, etc.);
- obtaining official transcripts directly from schools the candidate attended;
- obtaining driving records from state motor vehicle authorities;
- contracting with companies to obtain background investigations, criminal convictions checks, and credit checks (but be sure to comply with *Fair Credit Reporting Act* requirements); and,
- hiring candidates provided by employment agencies that pre-screen their referrals.

State governments are now beginning to address the related problem of *diploma mills*, which issue degrees based on little or no academic work. In Oregon, for example, it is illegal to claim to have an academic degree unless the degree is from an accredited school. Criminal and civil penalties can be imposed on persons who continue to claim such degrees after receiving a cease-and-desist notice from the Oregon state commission in charge of enforcing the law. North Dakota, New Jersey, and Indiana also have laws restricting claims to degrees from unaccredited schools.

The degree of thoroughness in verifying a candidate's résumé will depend on the position being filled. If the position involves access to the employer's money or to sensitive data, then a criminal convictions check and a credit check may be in order. Thoroughness will also be appropriate if the job poses a high risk of injury or loss to others. Examples might include resident managers, commercial drivers, heavy equipment operators, toxic waste handlers, armed security guards, health-care workers, bankers, stock brokers, locksmiths, or computer technicians. No list could possibly be exhaustive. The best approach is to consider the risks a particular employment position—any position—could present, and then make inquiries that are reasonable under the circumstances.

A written record of your inquiries should also be maintained. If the candidate is rejected based on information learned, the record will help defeat possible claims of discrimination. If the candidate is hired, the record will be useful in defending a claim of negligent hiring.

Third-Party Liability

Failure to make appropriate inquiries exposes the employer to direct loss due to the employee's lack of skill, carelessness, or intentional misconduct. It also could give rise to a claims of *vicarious liability* and *negligent hiring*.

As a matter of social policy, the law has long held employers liable to pay damages suffered by third parties due to an employee's negligent conduct that occurs within the scope of the employment. This type of indirect or vicarious liability to third parties is based on the legal doctrine known as *respondeat superior*—let the employer respond. It does not matter that the employer itself is guiltless or even that the employee acted contrary to the express instructions of his or her employer when the negligent conduct occurred.

The policy of imposing vicarious liability is based in part on the notion that, between the employer (who has the right to control its employees' conduct) and an innocent third party, the employer should bear the cost of the third party's injuries. The policy also recognizes that, for the most part, the employer is in a better position to pay damages or at least to assess the risks involved in the business and carry appropriate insurance.

Example

The store manager for drug store chain in Kansas was driving his own vehicle from his store to a district office of his employer to deliver football tickets given him by a vendor for distribution among the chain's managers. During the drive, he remembered that he needed to have some routine maintenance done on his car. He made a spur-of-the-moment decision to pull into a service station for an estimate, but while making a left turn into the service station, he failed to yield and collided with another car. The other driver sued both the manager and the drug store chain for his injuries.

A federal appeals court, applying Kansas law, ruled that a jury should have been allowed to find the chain vicariously liable. The court pointed out that the manager frequently used his personal vehicle for company business, he was still on the road to the district office when the accident occurred, and the time interval between the manager's departure from his specific duties and the accident was very brief. Given all these factors, said the court, a jury could reasonably conclude that the manager's departure was only a slight deviation—a mere detour—and not a personal frolic of his own.

O'Shea v. Welch, 350 F.3d 1101 (10th Cir. 2003)

Employers are usually not vicariously liable for their employees' *criminal conduct*, since such conduct is considered outside the scope of employment and undertaken solely for the employee's, not the employer's, benefit. However, if the employer places the employee in a position in which loss or damage to third parties could occur, and the employer fails to make adequate inquiry as to the employee's background, then the employer can be held liable for negligent hiring.

> **Example**
>
> An apartment building owner failed to perform a background check on a security guard it hired. Had it performed the check, it presumably would have discovered the guard's criminal conviction history. During the day of the incident in question, the guard helped a guest carry some packages to the apartment of a friend where she was staying. Later that day, the guard called the guest and asked if he could bring a gift. When the guest opened the apartment door, the guard sexually assaulted her. An Illinois appeals court ruled that the guest stated a good claim for negligent hiring.
>
> *Elliott v. Williams, 807 N.E.2d 506 (Ill.App. 2004)*

Remedies for Résumé Fraud

Suppose a falsified résumé slips past you and is not discovered until months or years later. What rights and remedies do you then have?

At-will employees may, of course, be discharged for any reason (except an illegal reason) or for no reason. If an employee has an employment contract, the résumé contains a false statement about some *material* matter (a matter that a reasonable person would find significant) and the employer relied on the statement in offering employment, then the employment contract is the product of the employee's misrepresentation. The employer may treat the contract as void and discharge the employee, as long as the employer acts promptly after discovering the misrepresentation.

On the other hand, if the false statement is an obvious typographical error (say, inversion of two digits in the date for previous employment), is trivial, or is so inherently improbable that the employer could not reasonably have relied on it, then the contract of employment remains enforceable.

Example

A Vermont businessman was convicted of bank fraud and sentenced to three years in federal prison. He was also ordered to pay restitution of $12 million. Upon his release from prison, he applied for a teaching position at a local community college. His résumé seemed to contain a complete work history, but it failed to mention the work he did while in prison and it stated that over the past few years he had been semi-retired. He also told the college he had a special interest and ability in teaching business law and ethics.

The college hired him on a one-year teaching contract, but fired him mid-year after learning of the conviction from his probation officer. The businessman then sued the college for breach of employment contract. On these facts the Vermont Supreme Court upheld the firing, saying that the businessman made material misrepresentations on which the college relied in making its employment decision. The court added that honesty is an implicit duty of every employee.

Sarvis v. Vermont State Colleges, 772 A.2d 494 (Vt. 2001)

Applications

Every employer needs its own individually designed *application for employment* for completion by all candidates. Typical subjects covered by an application include:

- ◆ candidate identification and contact information (name, address, Social Security number, and phone number);
- ◆ position for which the candidate is applying and how he or she learned of the position;
- ◆ candidate's education (if relevant to the job);
- ◆ candidate's experience and work history;
- ◆ licenses, certifications, or special skills, such as a commercial driver's license (if relevant to the job);
- ◆ certification that the candidate is eligible for employment (the candidate is at least 18 years old and is eligible to work in the U.S.);
- ◆ additional information as to eligibility (whether the candidate has previously worked for or applied to the company, been convicted of a serious crime, currently uses illegal drugs, is subject to a noncompete agreement with a prior employer, etc.); and,

♦ certification that the application is true and complete, and that related materials (résumé, transcripts, reference letters, etc.) are genuine and unaltered.

The candidate should not be asked to attach a photograph. Some seemingly innocuous application questions can also cause trouble. Age and/or birthdate questions should be saved until after the candidate has been hired to help avoid claims of age discrimination. For the same reason, dates of graduation should not be asked. (For child labor purposes, the employer should ask whether the candidate is at least 18.) Similarly, immigration status questions should be saved for later and the application should be limited to the question, *Are you legally eligible to work in the United States?* Even a question about who to contact in an emergency should be avoided in the initial application, since it could reveal marital status or family information not pertinent to the hiring process.

A sample application form (which needs to be tailored to suit each employer's individual situation) can be found on the following pages. Employers should also keep in mind that many states have special requirements and prohibitions regarding employment applications. Forms should therefore be reviewed and approved by experienced employment law counsel before being used.

Sample Employment Application

APPLICATION FOR EMPLOYMENT

The Company is an equal opportunity employer. All employment decisions, both during the hiring process and throughout the employment relationship, are based on merit alone, without regard to race, color, religion, sex, pregnancy, parenthood status, national origin, citizenship, age, marital status, disability, sexual orientation, or other prohibited criteria.

Please answer each of the following questions completely. If the question is not applicable to you, please indicate that by writing "Not Applicable" or "N/A." This application must be dated and signed in all places where indicated. The Company cannot consider this application unless every question is answered and it contains every required signature.

1. What is your full legal name? _____
2. What is your current mailing address?_____

_____

_____

3. What are your day and evening telephone numbers?_____

_____

4. What is your Social Security number? _____
5. Are you at least 18 years old? _____
6. Are you legally eligible to work in the United States? _____
7. What position you are applying for? _____
8. How did you become aware of this job opening? _____
9. When are you available to start work? _____
10. Did you graduate from high school? _____

(continued)

11. Have you had any formal education beyond high school? If yes, please describe, including names of schools attended and degrees received.

_____

_____

12. Please provide any additional information about your education that you believe makes you especially qualified for this position.

_____

_____

13. Have you previously been employed by this Company? If yes, please state the beginning and ending dates of employment and the name of your last supervisor. _____

_____

_____

14. Have you previously applied for employment by this Company? If yes, please state the date of your application and the position applied for.

_____

_____

15. Are you now employed? If yes, please provide the following information about your *current* employer:

    (a) Name _____

    (b) Address_____

    (c) Date you began work _____

    (d) Title and duties _____

    (e) Current salary or wages _____

    (f) Name of immediate supervisor_____

    (g) May we contact your supervisor for a reference?_____

    (h) If no, whom at your current employer may we contact? ____

    _____

    (i) Why do you want to leave your current job? _____

(continued)

16. Please provide the following information about your most recent *former* employer (not your current employer):

    (a) Name _____

    (b) Address_____

    (c) Beginning and ending dates of employment _____

    (d) Title and duties _____

    (e) Last salary or wages _____

    (f) Name of immediate supervisor_____

    (g) Reason for leaving _____

17. Please provide the following information about your *next most recent* former employer:

    (a) Name _____

    (b) Address_____

    (c) Beginning and ending dates of employment _____

    (d) Title and duties _____

    (e) Last salary or wages _____

    (f) Name of immediate supervisor_____

    (g) Reason for leaving _____

18. Please provide any additional information about your work history that you believe makes you especially qualified for this position.

_____

_____

19. Please describe any skills, certifications, licenses, hobbies, or interests not covered above that you believe makes you especially qualified for this position._____

_____

_____

_____

_____

(continued)

20. Have you been convicted of a crime within the last 10 years? (DO NOT INCLUDE CONVICTIONS THAT HAVE BEEN EXPUNGED.) If yes, please describe each conviction, including the date and place of conviction. _____

_____

_____

21. Do you currently hold a valid driver's license? If yes, in which state?

_____

22. Have you had your driver's license suspended or revoked within the last 10 years? If yes, please describe each suspension or revocation, including the date and the state involved. _____

_____

23. Do you currently use any illegal drugs? _____

24. Are you subject to any confidentiality agreements, noncompetition agreements, restrictive covenants, or similar agreements with your current employer or any previous employer? If yes, please describe and attach a copy. _____

_____

_____

25. Please give the names, addresses, and telephone numbers of three persons who know you and who have information about your work habits and abilities. Please state how long you have known each person and describe how you know him or her.

_____

_____

_____

_____

_____

(continued)

CERTIFICATIONS

I certify that the statements contained in my Application for Employment and in any résumé or similar document submitted in connection with my application for employment are true, correct and complete. I further certify that any transcript, certificate, reference letter or other document submitted in connection with my Application for Employment is genuine and has not been altered in any way. I understand that submitting false or incomplete information is grounds for termination.

I understand that, if offered employment and I accept, I may be required to undergo a medical examination at the Company's expense, including a test for current illegal drug use. Any offer of employment will be conditioned on my furnishing satisfactory evidence of my eligibility to work in the United States.

I understand that any employment that may be offered to me will be "at-will" employment only, meaning that I will not have a contract of employment and that the employment relationship can be terminated without cause at any time either by the Company or by me. I acknowledge that, as of the date of this application, I have not received any offers or promises of employment from the Company.

I acknowledge that this application will remain active only until (a) I am notified by the Company that I am no longer being considered for employment or (b) 60 days, whichever occurs first. Once this application becomes inactive, I will have to reapply for any job with the Company in which I may be interested.

_____   _____

[Today's date]   [Signature]

(continued)

AUTHORIZATION AND RELEASE

In connection with my application for employment, I authorize the release of information about my education, work experience, and fitness for employment by (a) schools I have attended; (b) my current and former employers; (c) employees and former employees of such employers; and, (d) my references. I release all persons and organizations from liability for furnishing information pursuant to this authorization.

_____   _____
[Today's date]   [Signature]

Background Checks

The federal *Fair Credit Reporting Act* (FCRA) regulates the obtaining and use of credit and investigative reports (which the statute refers to as *consumer reports*) by employers. The reports are prepared by *consumer reporting agencies*. The FCRA defines a *consumer reporting agency* (CRA) as a person or entity that, for a fee, assembles or evaluates credit information or other information on consumers for the purpose of regularly furnishing consumer reports to third parties (such as employers).

Employers may obtain consumer reports from CRAs—including investigative reports of character and general reputation—for purposes of evaluating a candidate for employment. In doing so employers must comply with the procedures specified in the FCRA.

When an employer intends to obtain a consumer report, the employer must inform the candidate in writing that such a report is being requested and must obtain the candidate's written authorization to obtain the report. The authorization should be a separate, stand-alone document and not be imbedded in the employment application or some other form. The candidate may in turn make a written request to be informed of the full nature and scope of the report being requested. The employer must then furnish that information.

If the employer intends to make an adverse employment decision based wholly or partly on the consumer report, the employer must first inform the candidate of its intention to do so. The employer must also furnish the candidate with the name and address of the CRA that made the report, a copy of the report, and a statement explaining the candidate's rights under federal law to challenge the accuracy of the report. The Federal Trade Commission, which enforces the FCRA, has developed a form statement of employee rights under federal law that satisfies the employer's FCRA obligations.

Prescribed Summary of Consumer Rights

The prescribed form for this summary is as a separate document, on paper no smaller than 8x11 inches in size, with text no less than 12-point type (8-point for the chart of federal agencies), in bold or capital letters as indicated. The form in this appendix prescribes both the content and the sequence of items in the required summary. A summary may accurately reflect changes in numerical items that change over time (*e.g.*, dollar amounts or phone numbers and addresses of federal agencies), and remain in compliance.

A SUMMARY OF YOUR RIGHTS
UNDER THE FAIR CREDIT REPORTING ACT

The federal *Fair Credit Reporting Act* (FCRA) is designed to promote accuracy, fairness, and privacy of information in the files of every consumer reporting agency (CRA). Most CRAs are credit bureaus that gather and sell information about you—such as if you pay your bills on time or have filed bankruptcy—to creditors, employers, landlords, and other businesses. You can find the complete text of the FCRA, 15 U.S.C. 1681-1681u, at the Federal Trade Commission's website (**www.ftc.gov**). The FCRA gives you specific rights, as outlined below. You may have addi-

(continued)

tional rights under state law. You may contact a state or local consumer protection agency or a state attorney general to learn those rights.

- **You must be told if information in your file has been used against you.** Anyone who uses information from a CRA to take action against you—such as denying an application for credit, insurance, or employment—must tell you, and give you the name, address, and phone number of the CRA that provided the consumer report.

- **You can find out what is in your file.** At your request, a CRA must give you the information in your file and a list of everyone who has requested it recently. There is no charge for the report if a person has taken action against you because of information supplied by the CRA, as long as you request the report within 60 days of receiving notice of the action. You also are entitled to one free report every twelve months upon request if you certify that (1) you are unemployed and plan to seek employment within 60 days; (2) you are on welfare; or, (3) your report is inaccurate due to fraud. Otherwise, a CRA may charge you up to $8.00.

- **You can dispute inaccurate information with the CRA.** If you tell a CRA that your file contains inaccurate information, the CRA must investigate the items (usually within 30 days) by presenting to its information source all relevant evidence you submit, unless your dispute is frivolous. The source must review your evidence and report its findings to the CRA. (The source also must advise national CRAs to which it has provided the data of any error.) The CRA must give you a written report of the investigation and a copy of your report if the investigation results in any change. If the CRA's investigation does not resolve the dispute, you may add a brief statement to your file. The CRA must

(continued)

normally include a summary of your statement in future reports. If an item is deleted or a dispute statement is filed, you may ask that anyone who has recently received your report be notified of the change.

- **Inaccurate information must be corrected or deleted.** A CRA must remove or correct inaccurate or unverified information from its files, usually within 30 days after you dispute it. *However, the CRA is not required to remove accurate data from your file unless it is outdated (as described below) or cannot be verified.* If your dispute results in any change to your report, the CRA cannot reinsert into your file a disputed item unless the information source verifies its accuracy and completeness. In addition, the CRA must give you a written notice telling you it has reinserted the item. The notice must include the name, address and phone number of the information source.

- **You can dispute inaccurate items with the source of the information.** If you tell anyone—such as a creditor who reports to a CRA—that you dispute an item, they may not then report the information to a CRA without including a notice of your dispute. In addition, once you've notified the source of the error in writing, it may not continue to report the information if it is, in fact, an error.

- **Outdated information may not be reported.** In most cases, a CRA may not report negative information that is more than seven years old (ten years for bankruptcies).

- **Access to your file is limited.** A CRA may provide information about you only to people with a need recognized by the FCRA—usually to consider an application with a creditor, insurer, employer, landlord, or other business.

(continued)

- **Your consent is required for reports that are provided to employers or reports that contain medical information.** A CRA may not give out information about you to your employer or prospective employer without your written consent. A CRA may not report medical information about you to creditors, insurers, or employers without your permission.

- **You may choose to exclude your name from CRA lists for unsolicited credit and insurance offers.** Creditors and insurers may use file information as the basis for sending you unsolicited offers of credit or insurance. Such offers must include a toll-free phone number for you to call if you want your name and address removed from future lists. If you call, you must be kept off the lists for two years. If you request, complete, and return the CRA form provided for this purpose, you must be taken off the lists indefinitely.

- **You may seek damages from violators.** If a user of or (in some cases) a provider of CRA data, or a CRA itself, violates the FCRA, you may sue them in state or federal court.

The FCRA gives several different federal agencies authority to enforce the FCRA.

FOR QUESTIONS OR CONCERNS REGARDING:	PLEASE CONTACT:
CRAs, creditors, and others not listed	Federal Trade Commission Consumer Response Center—FCRA Washington, DC 20580 877-382-4367

(continued)

National banks, federal branches/agencies of foreign banks (word National or initials N.A. appear in or after bank's name)	Office of the Comptroller of the Currency Compliance Management Mail Stop 6-6 Washington, DC 20219 800-613-6743
Federal Reserve System member banks (except national banks, and federal branches/agencies of foreign banks)	Federal Reserve Board Division of Consumer and Community Affairs Washington, DC 20551 202-452-3693
Savings associations and federally chartered savings banks (word Federal or initials F.S.B. appear in federal institution's name)	Office of Thrift Supervision Consumer Programs Washington, DC 20552 800-842-6929
Federal credit unions (words Federal Credit Union appear in institution's name)	National Credit Union Administration 1775 Duke Street Alexandria, VA 22314 703-518-6360
State-chartered banks that are not members of the Federal Deposit Insurance Corporation	Federal Reserve System Division of Compliance and Consumer Affairs Washington, DC 20429 800-934-FDIC

(continued)

Air, surface, or rail common carriers regulated by former Civil Aeronautics Board or Interstate Commerce Commission	Department of Transportation Office of Financial Management Washington, DC 20590 202-366-1306
Activities subject to the *Packers and Stockyards Act, 1921*	Department of Agriculture Office of Deputy Administrator—GIPSA Washington, DC 20250 202-720-7051

(A copy is also available from the FTC at **www.ftc.gov/os/statutes/ 2summary.htm**.)

Although the FCRA does not expressly require the employer to withhold an adverse decision until the candidate has had a chance to dispute negative information in the report, it is probably good practice for the employer to wait at least a brief time to see if the matter can be resolved. (Additional information about the FCRA is available at **www.ftc.gov/os/statutes/frcajump.htm**.)

If an employer decides that obtaining consumer reports is appropriate, the employer should identify those positions for which reports will be required and should be able to articulate business reasons justifying the requirement. The employer should also be sure that the policy is not implemented in a discriminatory manner.

10

Interviews

Good hiring practice involves the collection of appropriate information, untainted by information that should not be the basis for a hiring decision. The interview presents perhaps the most likely opportunity for an employer to acquire tainted information.

Interviews should be conducted by experienced personnel using a standard written interview form. The interview form should be limited to questions or topics directly relevant to job performance and the interviewer should stick to the form. By having and following a standard written form, the employer can more easily show that there was no inquiry about prohibited matters and that the candidate was not singled out for special questioning.

The interviewer should make written notes during the interview itself or promptly after it is concluded. Those notes, along with a copy of the employer's standard question set, should be retained.

Assuming the interview is conducted face-to-face, the candidate's race, color, and gender will usually be apparent; however, these are not suitable topics for discussion. During the interview itself, the candidate may volunteer information about his or her family status, political or religious affiliation, or union membership. The interviewer should not explore this volunteered information and, should the candidate bring the matter up again, the interviewer might even want to say that the company does not consider such matters when making employment decisions.

Disability-Related Questions

An employer may not ask, *"Are you disabled?"* or *"Do you have any medical conditions that could interfere with your performance?"* However, an employer may say, *"Can you do this job?"*—provided the question is asked of every candidate for this job and not just those who appear to have disabilities. The EEOC has prepared a long list of permitted and impermissible questions relating to disability discrimination. It can be found at **www.eeoc.gov/policy/docs/preemp.html**.

Open-Ended Questions

It is difficult to get a feel for a candidate's personality and communications skills if all he or she is asked are yes/no questions. To get to know the candidate better, interviewers naturally like to ask open-ended questions like *"Why do you want to work here?"* or *"Tell me what you like and do not like about your current job."* While open-ended questions such as these are perfectly proper and often helpful, open-ended questions that are not strictly job-related can be dangerous. They tend to elicit the very kind of information the employer does not want to know if it later must defend a discrimination claim.

Employer Misrepresentations

Interviews not only provide an opportunity for the employer to gather information about the candidate—they also allow the candidate to learn about the employer. Most employers will certainly want to put their best face forward, particularly for candidates on the short list. Employers need to be careful, however, that in doing so they do not *misrepresent* the position. When a candidate quits his or her existing job, turns down other offers, or moves across the country to accept new employment only to find out that the job is not what was promised, he or she can sue the employer for misrepresentation or deceit. The result may be a substantial damage award against the employer.

> ## Example
> Pierre worked for a multi-national sporting goods manufacturer in France. When a position with the company opened in Portland, Oregon, the company encouraged Pierre to apply. The company repeatedly stressed that it was looking for someone to stay in the position for at least two, preferably three years. Pierre, in turn, expressed the importance to him of job stability, particularly since he would be relocating with his wife and children and his wife would be taking leave from her existing job. The company failed to tell Pierre that it was considering moving the Portland position to Germany. After Pierre accepted the Portland position and began work, he discovered pressure within the company to move the position to Germany. Six months later, the company did in fact move the position to Germany and fired Pierre. A federal appeals court ruled that Pierre had a good suit for misrepresentation.
>
> *Arboireau v. Adidas-Salomon AG, 347 F.3d 1158 (9th Cir. 2003)*

Some employers have tried to escape liability in this situation by arguing that in an at-will employment relationship, the employer is free to terminate the employee at any time or to change the terms or conditions of employment. According to this argument, it does not matter that the job was misrepresented during pre-offer negotiations, because the employer could impose whatever new conditions it wished once the employment relationship had begun. The courts have responded by saying that the fact of an at-will relationship may affect the amount of damages a deceived employee can recover, but it does not bar him or her from suing in the first place.

Example

An account executive at a radio station in California who earned over $150,000 per year, was approached by a rival station. The executive responded that he would only consider a job as sales manager, which would pay overrides on sales by other salespersons, plus an equity interest in the station and a bonus plan. The executive explained that he had recently purchased a home and needed to make at least as much as he was currently earning. Ultimately, the parties reached an oral agreement that was reduced to writing, but the writing was silent on the length of employment. The account executive then resigned from his existing job and started work for the rival station.

Shortly thereafter, the executive's new employer told him he would be required to carry his own account list and that he would not be receiving overrides on other salespersons. The executive quit and sued for fraud and intentional misrepresentation. The station responded that since the executive was an at-will employee, his duties and compensation could be changed at any time, and he therefore suffered no damages.

An intermediate appellate court in California agreed that the executive was at will, but it ruled that the executive could still sue for damages. The court pointed out that the executive had not brought a wrongful discharge claim. Instead, he was suing for damages based on a claim that his new employer had no intention of meeting the offered employment terms in the first place and that the executive suffered damages when he left secure employment to take the new job.

Agosta v. Astor, 15 Cal. Rptr. 3d 565 (Cal.App. 2004)

Mindful of the risks associated with misrepresentation, employers should follow these guidelines when dealing with candidates on their short list.

- Describe the job accurately by furnishing a written job description that is complete and up-to-date.

- Give accurate estimates of job features that are likely to be of interest or concern to an employee, such as overtime requirements, travel, etc.

- Allow candidates an opportunity to review the employee handbook and other important policy statements with which they will be expected to comply if hired.

- Furnish copies of all agreements the candidate will be required to sign upon hiring, such as noncompete contracts and contracts that require arbitration of workplace disputes.

- Describe the hiring process, including who makes the decision to offer a job and what further approvals, if any, are necessary.

- State clearly and explicitly that the offer is conditioned on ratification by the company's board of directors or by some other official, if that is the case.

- Disclose all matters that could significantly affect the candidate's job, such as the company is about to move its facilities, is considering a possible bankruptcy, or is facing the loss of an important contract.

- Give the candidate a firm date by which the company will make a decision. If the company has not made a decision by that deadline, contact the candidate, inform him or her that the decision is still pending and ask if the candidate wishes to continue being considered.

- Once a decision is made, promptly inform the candidate.

- Send notes to any candidates being rejected, confirming the rejection and thanking them for their interest.

- Do not tell candidates that their applications will be kept on file and do not encourage them to think they are still under consideration when in fact they are not.

Testing

An employer may want candidates to take or undergo various tests as part of the interview and selection process. As discussed in following paragraphs, some tests are permitted, but must be used with care to avoid claims of discrimination. Other tests cannot be performed until an offer of employment has been made, and at least one type of test is illegal under almost all circumstances.

Title VII makes it unlawful for an employer, when selecting candidates for employment, to *adjust the scores of, use different cutoff scores for, or otherwise alter the results of, employment related tests on the basis of race, color, religion, sex, or national origin.* Even short of blatant discrimination such as using different cutoff scores, tests that have the unintended effect of excluding certain groups could result in *disparate impact discrimination.*

For enforcement purposes, the EEOC has adopted a *four-fifths rule.* If a particular test (or any other selection procedure, for that matter) excludes any race, gender, or ethnic group at a rate that is less than four-fifths that of the highest rate, the exclusion rate will be considered evidence of discrimination.

Tests also need to be *validated.* They must be shown by statistical or other evidence to be good predictors of job performance. The EEOC has adopted detailed regulations on validation requirements that go beyond the scope of this book. The regulations also require employers to keep records on the impact of their testing procedures, classified by gender, race, and ethnic group.

Medical and Drug Tests

Prior to actually offering employment, an employer may *never* require a candidate to undergo a medical exam. The only exception is testing for illegal drugs, which is not considered a medical exam and is permitted prior to making a job offer. Just about every other form of pre-offer medical test, including AIDS testing, genetic testing, and testing for the presence of alcohol, is illegal.

It is not always easy to determine whether a particular test is *medical* and therefore prohibited prior to making an offer of employment, or *non-medical* and therefore permitted. According to the EEOC, the following factors tend to make a particular test medical, and therefore prohibited *prior* to making an offer:

- if the test is administered by a *health-care professional* or someone trained by a health-care professional;
- if the test results are interpreted by a *health-care professional* or someone trained by a health-care professional;
- if the test is designed to reveal an *impairment, or physical or mental health*;
- if the employer is trying to determine the candidate's *physical or mental health or impairments*;
- if the test is *invasive* (for example, drawing blood, or taking a urine or breath specimen);
- if the test measures the candidate's *physiological responses* to performing a task (rather than just measuring the candidate's performance of the task;
- if the test is it normally given in a *medical setting* (for example, a health-care professional's office); or,
- if the test involves use of *medical equipment.*

(The EEOC has also provided examples of tests it considers medical and those it considers non-medical. See its website at **www.eeoc.gov/ policy/docs/preemp.html**.)

When the employer actually *offers* employment, the employer may condition the offer on the results of a medical exam if:

- all entering employees in the job category are subject to examination;
- the exam requirement can be shown to be job-related and consistent with business necessity;

◆ the resulting medical information is separately maintained and treated as confidential; and,

◆ the results are not used to discriminate against persons with disabilities.

Why would an employer want to condition an employment offer on passing a medical exam? Primarily, the employer wants to know that the employee can do the job. If the exam results show that the employee is incapable of doing the job and no reasonable accommodation is requested or possible, then the offer of employment will be withdrawn. If the exam results raise some doubt about the employee's ability, the employer might then want the employee's physician to certify that the employee is fit for duty or to identify any restrictions to which the employee is subject.

In addition, the employer will learn about any preexisting conditions. In the event the employee later suffers (or claims to have suffered) an on-the-job injury, knowledge of the preexisting condition may help the employer limit its liability for workers' compensation benefits.

Lie Detector Tests

With very limited exceptions, a federal law known as the *Employee Polygraph Protection Act* (EPPA) prohibits use of lie detectors in the hiring process. The term *lie detector* as used in the federal statute includes not only polygraph equipment (which measures pulse, respiration, and perspiration), but also any similar device, such as a voice stress analyzer. The EPPA even prohibits an employer from requesting or suggesting that a candidate submit to a lie detector test.

Exceptions to the EPPA include tests administered by federal, state, and local government employers and tests administered by the federal government to employees of government contractors in connection with security, counterintelligence, and law enforcement functions. In the private sector, prospective employees may be required to undergo lie detector tests in connection with employment as:

- armored car personnel;
- personnel engaged in the design, installation, and maintenance of security alarm systems; and,
- security personnel whose functions include protection of facilities that have a significant impact on public health or safety, such as nuclear power plants and the public water supply.

Offers and Rejections

Upon completion of the selection process, the next step is to make an offer of employment. Offers should be in writing to avoid confusion or misunderstanding. A typical offer letter might read similarly to the one on the following page.

A written rejection letter should be sent as well. The letter should thank the candidate for applying, but inform him or her in clear terms that the position is going to someone else and that he or she is no longer being considered. Statements to the effect of *your application is being kept on file for future reference* may soften the blow a bit, but they could mislead the candidate into thinking he or she is still in the running. If that mistaken belief causes the candidate to turn down another offer, a suit for misrepresentation may follow.

Sample Offer Letter

We are pleased to offer you the position of Sales Associate, beginning January 1, 2005. Your compensation will be in two components: the first component will be a base salary at the rate of $35,000 per year; the second component will be a commission computed and payable in accordance with the Company's Sales Associate Commission Plan, a copy of which is attached. The Company reserves the right to change the Commission Plan at any time.

This offer is subject to your furnishing sufficient evidence that you are legally eligible to work in the United States and to your undergoing a medical examination at the company's expense.

Vacation and sick leave policies, benefit plans, and other Company rules and policies are explained in our Employee Handbook, a copy of which will be given to you on your start date. You are expected to read and be familiar with the Employee Handbook.

This letter is not intended to be a contract of employment. You will be an at-will employee of the Company, meaning that either you or the Company can terminate the employment relationship at any time for any reason, with or without good cause.

If you accept this offer, please sign and return the enclosed copy of this letter no later than December 17, 2004.

You should report January 3rd at 8:30 a.m. as your first day of work to complete the hiring process.

We look forward to having you with us!

11

Contracts of Employment

Now that you have made a written offer to the candidate of your choice and he or she has accepted that offer, you need to take appropriate steps to bring your new employee on board.

At-Will and Contract Employees

One of the first decisions you must make is whether your new employee will be *at will* or whether you will offer him or her an *employment contract*. In most states, unless the employer and employee agree otherwise, the employment relationship is at will. This means that either party—employer or employee—can terminate the relationship at any time for any reason (except an illegal reason) or for no reason at all. In other words, an employer does not need good cause to fire an at-will employee, and an at-will employee does not need good cause to quit. (see Chapter 14.)

On the other hand, if the parties to the relationship enter into a contract of employment that specifies how the relationship may be terminated, then the employment is no longer at will and the terms of the contract govern. A contract that says the employment will last three years, for example, or that the employment may only be terminated for cause, overrides the normal, at-will relationship. So does a contract that allows the employee to invoke a grievance procedure or that establishes a binding progressive discipline policy.

Collective bargaining agreements between employers and unions are good examples of contracts that alter the at-will employment relationship.

Not all contracts between an employer and an employee affect the employee's at-will status. Noncompete agreements and arbitration agreements, for example, deal with certain aspects of the employment relationship without necessarily promising a specific term of employment or a right to fire only for cause. It is a good idea, however, whenever an employer and an employee enter into any kind of written arrangement, to state explicitly that the arrangement is not intended to alter the employee's at-will status, if that is what is intended.

Preserving At-Will Status

For a variety of reasons, employers will normally want to keep their employees in an at-will status. Primarily, employers feel that having the absolute power to fire helps maintain discipline in the workplace and control over their workers. Second, employers have greater flexibility in altering the terms and conditions of employment. The power to terminate the relationship entirely necessarily implies the power to change assignments, to add or eliminate duties, to modify or cancel benefit plans, and even to reduce compensation.

From an employer's perspective, employment contracts are often unattractive for the additional reason that, as a practical matter, they tend to be one-sided. If the *employer* violates the contract by firing the employee contrary to the terms of the contract, the employee can sue for damages. The employee's damages in that case will usually be the amount of compensation and benefits the employee would have received under the contract but for being fired, less any amounts the employee earns or could have earned during the remaining contract period.

In contrast, if the *employee* violates the contract by quitting, the employer can sue for damages, but the employer may have a difficult time proving the amount of damages it suffered by reason of the employee's breach. Further, an employer cannot force the employee to return to work, since both the Thirteenth Amendment to the U.S. Constitution and federal law outlaw compulsory labor.

An important corollary of the at-will doctrine has to do with the *implied covenant of good faith and fair dealing.* In most states, every contract is presumed to contain that implied covenant, so that parties to the contract must act reasonably toward each other. However, with a few exceptions, the covenant is not implied in the normal at-will employment arrangement, since the covenant depends on the existence of an employment contract with a definite term.

Example

A life insurance agent in West Virginia had a contract with his insurance company employer specifying that he was an at-will employee. After eight years on the job he was fired, allegedly to prevent him from collecting certain renewal commissions on policies he had previously sold. The agent sued for the commissions, claiming that by firing him, the company breached an implied covenant of good faith and fair dealing. The West Virginia Supreme Court denied the agent's claim, ruling that the implied covenant is not recognized in an at-will employment contract.

Miller v. Massachusetts Mut. Life Ins. Co., 455 S.E.2d 799 (W.Va. 1995)

There may be times when an employer is voluntarily willing to offer job security. The labor market may be tight, for example, and the employer may be having trouble attracting qualified candidates. Or a highly desirable candidate may insist on a contract as a condition to accepting an offer, particularly if the candidate is giving up a secure position, is moving across the country to take the job, or is turning down another offer.

Contents of Contract

The contents of any particular employment contract will depend on the circumstances. A typical contract might include provisions dealing with:

- title and brief summary of duties;
- beginning and ending dates of employment and whether the contract may be extended;
- compensation arrangements;
- bonuses and stock options;
- health and other benefit plans;
- other fringe benefits (company car, expense account, etc.);
- exclusivity (whether the employee may moonlight);
- prohibition on conflicts of interest;
- any unique vacation or sick leave arrangements;
- grounds for early termination (*e.g.*, death, disability, or good cause);
- a definition of *good cause* if it is a ground for early termination;
- duty of confidentiality;
- restriction on competing after termination of the contract;
- prohibition against soliciting customers and fellow employees after termination of the contract;
- ownership of intellectual property (copyrightable works and patentable inventions); and,
- arbitration of disputes.

Fill-in-the-blank contract forms are available from commercial publishers. Electronic forms can even be purchased or downloaded from the Internet, edited, and printed. But if the employment relationship is important enough to justify a contract in the first place, it should be important enough to justify a consultation with employment counsel to be sure the contract fits the particular circumstances and conforms with local law.

Employee Handbooks

It would be difficult to overstate the benefits of having an employee handbook. Handbooks promote uniformity in treatment of employees, particularly for larger employers with several layers of management. That, in turn, improves morale and frees the employer from a stream of requests for special treatment.

Handbooks are also a convenient source of information for job candidates and new hires, as well as existing employees. They promote efficiency and they help to establish an institutional culture. They set out rules of workplace behavior that, if willfully violated and result in termination, provide the employer with a defense to an unemployment insurance claim or an abusive discharge suit. Finally, they provide evidence of employer compliance with law in areas such as workers' compensation, equal employment, and sexual harassment.

An outline of the contents of a typical employee handbook is set out in Appendix B. Employers who choose to have an employee handbook should be aware that if the handbook describes leave policies and the employer is covered by the *Family and Medical Leave Act* (FMLA), the handbook *must* include a description of extended leave benefits under FMLA.

When distributing employee handbooks to new employees, the employee should sign an acknowledgment that he or she has received the handbook and will read it. Such acknowledgments are helpful in meeting an employee's claim that he or she was unaware of a particular policy or procedure contained in the handbook.

The down side is that an employee handbook or similar statement of policy might be considered an implied contract of employment that effectively converts all your at-will employment relationships to contractual relationships.

Example

After some four years on the job as Director of Public Affairs for a health-care plan in the District of Columbia, Stephanie was fired over

(continued)

---

her refusal to enroll in the company's career reappraisal program. At the time of Stephanie's termination, the company's personnel policies manual provided for a progressive discipline policy, which described specific steps to be followed prior to termination of employment. Although there was a disclaimer in the introduction of the manual indicating that it was not a contract, other language in the manual used mandatory terms in setting forth various conditions of employment. There was also a declaration that the manual was a statement of the company's intention in matters covered by the policy.

Stephanie sued, claiming that the manual constituted an implied contract of employment, which the company breached by firing her without following its progressive disciplinary policy. The company asked the court to dismiss the suit on grounds that the disclaimer conclusively established that the manual was not a contract. The court ruled that the disclaimer was not legally sufficient to overcome the contractual nature of the handbook and it upheld a jury verdict in Stephanie's favor.

Strass v. Kaiser Foundation Health Plan of Mid-Atlantic, 744 A.2d 1000 (D.C. 2000)

An employer who wishes to adopt an employee handbook but who does not want to be contractually bound by its provisions can take steps to reduce, if not eliminate, the risk of contractual liability.

- ◆ Include prominent disclaimers that the handbook is not a contract of employment and is not intended to change the at-will status of any employee.
- ◆ State that the handbook is intended only as a convenient source of information about the company and its current practices and procedures, which are subject to change at any time without prior notice.

◆ State that employees are free to resign and that the company is free to discharge an employee at any time, with or without cause.

◆ State that the company is not bound to follow any particular disciplinary procedures and that the company need not be consistent in imposing discipline.

◆ Avoid statements such as the company *promises, guarantees,* or *will* take specified action in certain circumstances.

◆ Do not require employees to *sign an agreement* to comply with or be bound by the handbook.

12

Noncompete and Other Agreements

Depending on the type of business you operate, it may be appropriate for you to require certain incoming employees to sign one or more agreements discussed in this chapter. While these agreements are not intended to alter the at-will status of your employees, they do affect other aspects of the employment relationship and they impose obligations on your employees after their employment terminates.

As a matter of general contract law, all agreements require *consideration* to be enforceable. That is, each party to the agreement must get something of value from the other party in exchange for (*in consideration of*) the promises he or she is making. The same is true of employment-related agreements. In most states, merely employing the employee is sufficient consideration to support whatever promises the employee makes in the agreements discussed here.

Certain types of agreements will not be enforceable by the courts, even though they are supported by consideration. To illustrate, an employee cannot be asked to give up in advance his or her right to file a charge of discrimination with the Equal Employment Opportunity Commission should sexual harassment or some other form of workplace discrimination occur later. Nor can a nonexempt employee agree to work for less than the minimum wage or give up a claim to overtime pay for work in excess of forty hours per week. A contract of *involuntary servitude* that attempts to force an employee to work for a particular employer is not enforceable, because the law no longer recognizes the status of indentured servant.

The agreements discussed here will generally be upheld in the courts, as long as their terms are reasonable and they do not try to restrict or take away rights guaranteed by law to employees.

Noncompete Agreements

While in your employ, your employees owe you a *duty of loyalty*. Among other things, this means that they cannot actively compete with you, such as by servicing your customers directly in their off hours or by passing leads to your competitor. But once the employment ends, your former employees are free to go to work for the competition or start competing businesses of their own. *Noncompete agreements* (sometimes called *restrictive covenants*) fill this gap by prohibiting your former employees from competing after their employment ends.

It would be nice if you could force every new employee, from the senior vice-president down to the cleaning crew, to a sign noncompete agreement. That way, their ability to leave you for new jobs would be severely restricted and you would in effect have a captive workforce. But the law does not grant employers such unfettered power over their workers. A noncompete agreement may be used to prevent *unfair competition*—it cannot be used to gain an *unfair advantage*.

When might an employer appropriately insist on the protection of a noncompete agreement? Examples include:

- ◆ *sales positions*, when the business is heavily dependent on the relationship between the salesperson and his or her customers and the customers would likely follow the salesperson to a new employer;

♦ *professional practices*, when the clients or patients tend to identify with particular professionals in the firm and not with the firm as a whole;

♦ jobs for which the employer must make a *substantial initial investment* in the employee's education or training, or when the employee is unproductive while awaiting a security clearance or a special license or certification;

♦ jobs requiring *unique skill sets*;

♦ jobs involving access to *highly confidential trade secrets*; and,

♦ *high-tech positions* in which the employee is likely to generate or have access to intellectual property such as computer programs or patentable devices.

To be enforceable, the restrictions imposed by a noncompete agreement must be *reasonable*. Traditionally, the courts have looked to these three factors in determining reasonableness:

1. the particular work that the employee is prohibited from doing;
2. the geographic area in which he or she is barred from competing; and,
3. the duration of the restriction.

The reasonableness requirement arises largely because a by-product of every noncompete agreement is a limitation on the employee's ability to find work and support him- or herself and his or her family. The general public also has an interest in free competition. If your employee really can provide a product or service that is better, cheaper, and more reliable than yours, the public would certainly want him or her to be free to do so. Drawing the line between reasonable and unreasonable is a case-by-case process, and it is difficult to say in advance whether any particular agreement is likely to be upheld by the courts or to be found over-broad.

The geographic restriction factor may be disappearing in certain cases. As information technology assumes a greater role in the economy and as the speed and ease of communications increase, it makes little difference whether, for example, a computer programmer works in his or her employer's office, in the employee's own mountain retreat, or in Bangalore, India. Merely prohibiting the programmer from competing within a ten-mile radius of the office will not be very effective.

> ## Example
> An employer headquartered in Maryland was in the business of developing, selling, and supporting software products for health-care organizations on a global basis. Its account managers were required to sign noncompete agreements that did not contain any geographical restriction. When an account manager, who mostly worked out of his home in Michigan, left the company and went to work for a competitor in Ohio, the Maryland company sued for an injunction prohibiting the new employment. The court granted the injunction, noting that a restrictive covenant limited to a narrow geographic area would render the restriction meaningless.
>
> *Intelus Corp. v. Barton, 7 F. Supp. 2d 635 (D.Md.1998)*

Nonsolicitation Agreements

When an employee leaves with the intention of going into competition with his or her former employer, he or she will likely plan to contact former customers and invite them to become customers of the new business. Similarly, he or she will likely try to induce fellow employees to come work at the new business. A standard provision in noncompete agreements is a prohibition on soliciting customers and fellow employees.

A nonsolicitation provision may prohibit the departing employee from servicing *all* clients of the employer, not just the clients of the employer with whom the employee had contact or with whom he or she worked. A nonsolicitation provision may even be applied to customers that the employee brought with him or her, since relationships with those customers become part of the employer's goodwill. Unlike noncompete clauses, in most states a nonsolicitation provision need not be limited in duration or by geography, although some courts impose the same reasonableness requirements on nonsolicitation agreements as they do on noncompete agreements.

Confidentiality Agreements

As a supplement to common-law duties of loyalty, most states have adopted the *Uniform Trade Secrets Act* (UTSA). This Act prohibits the *misappropriation of trade secrets by improper means*. *Trade secret* is defined as information that has economic value because it is not generally known to others and that the employer makes reasonable efforts to keep secret. *Improper means* includes theft, bribery, misrepresentation, breach of duty to maintain secrecy, and espionage. If an employee steals information or documents while still employed— say, in anticipation of leaving that job and going with a competitor—the company will have a claim against him or her under the UTSA. Theft of a trade secret is also criminal under the federal *Economic Espionage Act.*

Confidentiality agreements supplement the UTSA in important ways. In a typical confidentiality agreement, the employee will acknowledge that all company information, customer lists, cost structures, etc., belong to the company, and will promise to maintain the confidentiality of that information throughout his or her employment and after the employment ends. Such agreements demonstrate that the employer is making reasonable efforts to keep information confidential, thus bringing the information within the definition of *trade secret* under the UTSA. Such agreements also impose a duty to maintain secrecy, so that breach of a confidentiality agreement may in certain circumstances be a violation of the statute as well.

As with nonsolicitation agreements, confidentiality agreements may last for an indefinite period, or at least until the confidential information becomes known to the public generally.

Intellectual Property

Who owns the rights to a device invented by your employee or to an instruction manual written by your employee—you or your employee? In general, the right to patent an invention belongs to the inventor personally and ownership of the copyright of a work belongs to the author personally. There is an exception under federal copyright law for a *work made for hire*—defined as a work prepared by an employee within the scope of his or her employment—but there is no similar exception under the patent law for inventions. Even with copyrightable works, a question can arise whether a particular work was prepared within or outside the scope of the employee's employment. In short, when an employer hires someone to work on a potentially patentable invention or a copyrightable work, the employer needs greater protection than federal law provides.

The solution is to have the employee sign an agreement that all inventions and works created during employment, and for some reasonable period after the employment ends, are considered made for hire and belong to the employer. Such agreements usually contain an express assignment of all rights to the employer.

Arbitration Agreements

Arbitration of disputes is often viewed as preferable to litigation. Arbitration is—or at least it is perceived to be—faster and cheaper. It involves only limited pretrial discovery, the proceedings take place in private, and the results are usually final and unappealable. Since arbitration means no jury trial, an employer who fears a runaway jury and a runaway damage award may view arbitration as a highly desirable alternative to litigation.

Both the *Federal Arbitration Act* (FAA) and its state counterparts say that a contract provision for resolution of future disputes by arbitration is valid and enforceable. The courts have gone so far as to rule that the law favors arbitration, and that when a contract contains an arbitration clause, a presumption arises that all disputes relating to the contract must be arbitrated.

For some time there was a question whether an employee could be forced to arbitrate his or her *federal statutory claims*, such as claims of discrimination under *Title VII* of the *Civil Rights Act*. The Supreme Court resolved the question in March 2001. In a decision involving an employee of an electronics store in California, the Court ruled that an agreement to arbitrate discrimination claims was valid and enforceable under the FAA. The Court went on to praise arbitration agreements in employment, saying that they allow parties to avoid the costs of litigation—a benefit that may be of particular importance in employment litigation, which often involves smaller sums of money than disputes concerning commercial contracts.

The Equal Employment Opportunity Commission, which opposes binding arbitration of discrimination claims, is not stopped from investigating or attempting to reconcile a discrimination charge just because the parties have entered into an arbitration agreement. In a recent case, a restaurant employee was fired from his short-order cook job when the restaurant learned he suffered from seizures. In response to the EEOC's suit for violations of the *Americans with Disabilities Act*, the restaurant argued that the employee had signed a predispute arbitration agreement that barred the EEOC's suit. The Supreme Court upheld the EEOC's suit, saying the EEOC has an independent statutory right to pursue whatever remedies it feels appropriate, including so-called victim-specific relief such as reinstatement, backpay, and compensatory and punitive damages.

Arbitration may not always be cheaper than litigation—at least from the employee's perspective. Keep in mind that it costs nothing to file a discrimination charge with the EEOC or with a state fair employment practices agency (FEPA). If the matter is not resolved at that level, the employee can go to court simply by paying a modest filing fee. While the employee may have to pay his or her own attorney on an hourly or some other basis, those attorneys' fees can be recovered if the employee ultimately wins. The judge's services are provided for free, since the judge is a salaried government employee.

In contrast, there are substantial filing fees just to initiate arbitration. Since the arbitrator is not a salaried government employee, the parties, or at least one of them, will have to pay his or her fee. And unless the arbitration agreement says otherwise, the employee normally pays his or her own attorney without any right to reimbursement, even if he or she wins.

Some employers have tried to shift the burden of arbitration costs to the employee, so that the employee ends up paying far more to arbitrate than he or she would to sue in court. Other employers have drafted arbitration agreements that are so one-sided in favor of the employer as to be fundamentally unfair to the employee. A number of federal appellate courts have refused to enforce such agreements, ruling that any attempt to burden an employee with excessive costs or to give employers unfair procedural advantages is a denial of the employee's statutory rights.

The American Arbitration Association (AAA), which has its own set of rules for resolving employment disputes, will not arbitrate a dispute if the underlying agreement does not assure minimal standards of fairness to the employee. (The AAA's procedural rules and guidelines for the various types of disputes it handles may be found at **www.adr.org**.)

Another private organization, known as JAMS (formerly Judicial Arbitration and Mediation Service), also handles employment matters. (Information on this organization can be obtained at **www.jamsadr.com**.)

Despite the Supreme Court's blessing, legal issues involved in predispute arbitration agreements continue to develop, particularly in the area of fairness and cost-shifting. While there can be no guarantees, following these steps should help to assure the validity of such agreements.

- ◆ The agreement should contain a *clear and unmistakable waiver* of the employee's right to go to court, and should specify that arbitration is *final and binding.*

- ◆ The agreement should specifically identify the types of potential claims that the employer intends to submit to arbitration. These would include claims under *Title VII*, the ADA, the ADEA, state human rights and fair employment practices acts, and county and local nondiscrimination laws, as well as claims for abusive discharge, pay disputes, and so on.

- ◆ The agreement should not burden the employee with costs significantly in excess of the costs he or she would incur in court.

- ◆ The agreement should be balanced, fair to both sides, and should not attempt to give the employer any procedural advantages.

- ◆ Finally, the agreement should not attempt to take away any of the employee's substantive statutory rights or to limit an employee's statutory remedies.

For companies that require employees to sign noncompetition or nonsolicitation clauses, an arbitration agreement should have an exception allowing the employer to go to court for an injunction to bar an employee's or former employee's violation of the clause.

Union Shops

Federal labor law makes it an unfair labor practice for a unionized employer to refuse to bargain collectively with its unions. The term *bargain collectively* is defined as *the performance of the mutual obligation of the employer and the representative of the employees to meet at reasonable times and confer in good faith with respect to wages, hours, and other terms and conditions of employment.* One of the issues that is likely to come up in contract negotiations is *union security*—that is, whether all eligible employees must join the union upon hiring (a *union shop*) or must at least pay dues to the union (an *agency shop*).

Federal labor law permits union shop and agency shop agreements between employers and unions. However, federal labor law also permits individual states to enact so-called *right-to-work* laws, making union security agreements illegal in those states.

Some twenty-three states have done exactly that. At this writing, the following states have right-to-work provisions in their state constitutions or statutes:

Alabama	Nevada
Arizona	Nebraska
Arkansas	North Carolina
Florida	North Dakota
Georgia	Oklahoma
Idaho	South Carolina
Indiana	South Dakota
(only applicable to school employees)	Tennessee
Iowa	Texas
Kansas	Utah
Louisiana	Virginia
Mississippi	Wyoming

(For a current listing of right-to-work states, go to **www.dol.gov/esa/ programs/whd/state/righttowork.htm**.)

Suppose an employee in a union or agency shop holds religious or moral convictions against union participation. Federal law provides a limited escape clause. It says that any employee who is a member of and adheres to established and traditional tenets or teachings of a *bona fide* religion, body, or sect that has historically held conscientious objections to joining or financially supporting labor organizations, may, instead of paying union dues, pay an equal amount to a designated charity.

13

Requirements Applicable to New Employees

W hether or not you enter into formal contracts of employment and whether or not you require your employees to sign noncompete, arbitration, or similar agreeements are matters of business judgment. In contrast, the requirements discussed in this chapter are not optional and they must be satisfied with respect to each new employee.

I-9 REQUIREMENTS

It is illegal to knowingly hire, recruit, refer for a fee, or continue to employ persons who are not eligible to work in the United States. Ignorance of the employee's status is no excuse. Employers are required to establish the eligibility of *every new employee* by having the employee exhibit certain documents and by completing and retaining a federally-mandated Form I-9. A copy of Form I-9 and instructions, promulgated by the United States Citizenship and Immigration Services (USCIS) of the Department of Homeland Security (formerly the Immigration and Naturalization Service of the Department of Justice) can be found on the following pages. (It is also available at **http://uscis.gov/graphics/formsfee/forms/index.htm**.)

U.S. Department of Justice	OMB No. 1115-0136
Immigration and Naturalization Service	**Employment Eligibility Verification**

INSTRUCTIONS
PLEASE READ ALL INSTRUCTIONS CAREFULLY BEFORE COMPLETING THIS FORM.

Anti-Discrimination Notice. It is illegal to discriminate against any individual (other than an alien not authorized to work in the U.S.) in hiring, discharging, or recruiting or referring for a fee because of that individual's national origin or citizenship status. It is illegal to discriminate against work eligible individuals. Employers **CANNOT** specify which document(s) they will accept from an employee. The refusal to hire an individual because of a future expiration date may also constitute illegal discrimination.

Section 1 - Employee.
All employees, citizens and noncitizens, hired after November 6, 1986, must complete Section 1 of this form at the time of hire, which is the actual beginning of employment. **The employer is responsible for ensuring that Section 1 is timely and properly completed.**

Preparer/Translator Certification. The Preparer/Translator Certification must be completed if Section 1 is prepared by a person other than the employee. A preparer/translator may be used only when the employee is unable to complete Section 1 on his/her own. However, the employee must still sign Section 1.

Section 2 - Employer.
For the purpose of completing this form, the term "employer" includes those recruiters and referrers for a fee who are agricultural associations, agricultural employers or farm labor contractors.

Employers must complete Section 2 by examining evidence of identity and employment eligibility within three (3) business days of the date employment begins. If employees are authorized to work, but are unable to present the required document(s) within three business days, they must present a receipt for the application of the document(s) within three business days and the actual document(s) within ninety (90) days. However, if employers hire individuals for a duration of less than three business days, Section 2 must be completed at the time employment begins. **Employers must record: 1)** document title; 2) issuing authority; 3) document number, **4)** expiration date, if any; and 5) the date employment begins. Employers must sign and date the certification. Employees must present original documents. Employers may, but are not required to, photocopy the document(s) presented. These photocopies may only be used for the verification process and must be retained with the I-9. **However, employers are still responsible for completing the I-9.**

Section 3 - Updating and Reverification.
Employers must complete Section 3 when updating and/or reverifying the I-9. Employers must reverify employment eligibility of their employees on or before the expiration date recorded in Section 1. Employers **CANNOT** specify which document(s) they will accept from an employee.

- If an employee's name has changed at the time this form is being updated/ reverified, complete Block A.

- If an employee is rehired within three (3) years of the date this form was originally completed and the employee is still eligible to be employed on the same basis as previously indicated on this form (updating), complete Block B and the signature block.

- If an employee is rehired within three (3) years of the date this form was originally completed and the employee's work authorization has expired or if a current employee's work authorization is about to expire (reverification), complete Block B and:
  - examine any document that reflects that the employee is authorized to work in the U.S. (see List A or C),
  - record the document title, document number and expiration date (if any) in Block C, and complete the signature block.

Photocopying and Retaining Form I-9. A blank I-9 may be reproduced, provided both sides are copied. The Instructions must be available to all employees completing this form. Employers must retain completed I-9s for three (3) years after the date of hire or one (1) year after the date employment ends, whichever is later.

For more detailed information, you may refer to the INS Handbook for Employers, (Form M-274). You may obtain the handbook at your local INS office.

Privacy Act Notice. The authority for collecting this information is the Immigration Reform and Control Act of 1986, Pub. L. 99-603 (8 USC 1324a).

This information is for employers to verify the eligibility of individuals for employment to preclude the unlawful hiring, or recruiting or referring for a fee, of aliens who are not authorized to work in the United States.

This information will be used by employers as a record of their basis for determining eligibility of an employee to work in the United States. The form will be kept by the employer and made available for inspection by officials of the U.S. Immigration and Naturalization Service, the Department of Labor and the Office of Special Counsel for Immigration Related Unfair Employment Practices.

Submission of the information required in this form is voluntary. However, an individual may not begin employment unless this form is completed, since employers are subject to civil or criminal penalties if they do not comply with the Immigration Reform and Control Act of 1986.

Reporting Burden. We try to create forms and instructions that are accurate, can be easily understood and which impose the least possible burden on you to provide us with information. Often this is difficult because some immigration laws are very complex. Accordingly, the reporting burden for this collection of information is computed as follows: 1) learning about this form, 5 minutes; 2) completing the form, 5 minutes; and 3) assembling and filing (recordkeeping) the form, 5 minutes, for an average of 15 minutes per response. If you have comments regarding the accuracy of this burden estimate, or suggestions for making this form simpler, you can write to the Immigration and Naturalization Service, HQPDI, 425 I Street, N.W., Room 4307r, Washington, DC 20536. OMB No. 1115-0136.

EMPLOYERS MUST RETAIN COMPLETED FORM I-9
PLEASE DO NOT MAIL COMPLETED FORM I-9 TO INS

Form I-9 (Rev. 11-21-91)N

U.S. Department of Justice
Immigration and Naturalization Service

OMB No. 1115-0136

Employment Eligibility Verification

Please read instructions carefully before completing this form. The instructions must be available during completion of this form. ANTI-DISCRIMINATION NOTICE: It is illegal to discriminate against work eligible individuals. Employers CANNOT specify which document(s) they will accept from an employee. The refusal to hire an individual because of a future expiration date may also constitute illegal discrimination.

Section 1. Employee Information and Verification. To be completed and signed by employee at the time employment begins.

Print Name: Last	First	Middle Initial	Maiden Name

Address *(Street Name and Number)*	Apt. #	Date of Birth *(month/day/year)*

City	State	Zip Code	Social Security #

I am aware that federal law provides for imprisonment and/or fines for false statements or use of false documents in connection with the completion of this form.

I attest, under penalty of perjury, that I am (check one of the following):
- [ ] A citizen or national of the United States
- [ ] A Lawful Permanent Resident (Alien # A_____)
- [ ] An alien authorized to work until ___/___/___
  (Alien # or Admission #) _____

Employee's Signature	Date *(month/day/year)*

Preparer and/or Translator Certification. *(To be completed and signed if Section 1 is prepared by a person other than the employee.) I attest, under penalty of perjury, that I have assisted in the completion of this form and that to the best of my knowledge the information is true and correct.*

Preparer's/Translator's Signature	Print Name

Address *(Street Name and Number, City, State, Zip Code)*	Date *(month/day/year)*

Section 2. Employer Review and Verification. To be completed and signed by employer. Examine one document from List A OR examine one document from List B and one from List C, as listed on the reverse of this form, and record the title, number and expiration date, if any, of the document(s)

List A	OR	List B	AND	List C
Document title: _____		_____		_____
Issuing authority: _____		_____		_____
Document #: _____		_____		_____
Expiration Date *(if any)*: ___/___/___		___/___/___		___/___/___
Document #: _____				
Expiration Date *(if any)*: ___/___/___				

CERTIFICATION - I attest, under penalty of perjury, that I have examined the document(s) presented by the above-named employee, that the above-listed document(s) appear to be genuine and to relate to the employee named, that the employee began employment on *(month/day/year)* ___/___/___ and that to the best of my knowledge the employee is eligible to work in the United States. (State employment agencies may omit the date the employee began employment.)

Signature of Employer or Authorized Representative	Print Name	Title

Business or Organization Name	Address *(Street Name and Number, City, State, Zip Code)*	Date *(month/day/year)*

Section 3. Updating and Reverification. To be completed and signed by employer.

A. New Name *(if applicable)*	B. Date of rehire *(month/day/year)* *(if applicable)*

C. If employee's previous grant of work authorization has expired, provide the information below for the document that establishes current employment eligibility.

Document Title: _____   Document #: _____   Expiration Date (if any): ___/___/___

I attest, under penalty of perjury, that to the best of my knowledge, this employee is eligible to work in the United States, and if the employee presented document(s), the document(s) I have examined appear to be genuine and to relate to the individual.

Signature of Employer or Authorized Representative	Date *(month/day/year)*

Form I-9 (Rev. 11-21-91)N Page 2

LISTS OF ACCEPTABLE DOCUMENTS

LIST A		LIST B		LIST C
Documents that Establish Both Identity and Employment Eligibility	**OR**	**Documents that Establish Identity**	**AND**	**Documents that Establish Employment Eligibility**

LIST A — Documents that Establish Both Identity and Employment Eligibility

1. U.S. Passport (unexpired or expired)

2. Certificate of U.S. Citizenship *(INS Form N-560 or N-561)*

3. Certificate of Naturalization *(INS Form N-550 or N-570)*

4. Unexpired foreign passport, with *I-551 stamp or* attached *INS Form I-94* indicating unexpired employment authorization

5. Alien Registration Receipt Card with photograph *(INS Form I-151 or I-551)*

6. Unexpired Temporary Card *(INS Form I-688)*

7. Unexpired Employment Authorization Card *(INS Form I-688A)*

8. Unexpired Reentry Permit *(INS Form I-327)*

9. Unexpired Refugee Travel Document *(INS Form I-571)*

10. Unexpired Employment Authorization Document issued by the INS which contains a photograph *(INS Form I-688B)*

LIST B — Documents that Establish Identity

1. Driver's license or ID card issued by a state or outlying possession of the United States provided it contains a photograph or information such as name, date of birth, sex, height, eye color and address

2. ID card issued by federal, state or local government agencies or entities, provided it contains a photograph or information such as name, date of birth, sex, height, eye color and address

3. School ID card with a photograph

4. Voter's registration card

5. U.S. Military card or draft record

6. Military dependent's ID card

7. U.S. Coast Guard Merchant Mariner Card

8. Native American tribal document

9. Driver's license issued by a Canadian government authority

For persons under age 18 who are unable to present a document listed above:

10. School record or report card

11. Clinic, doctor or hospital record

12. Day-care or nursery school record

LIST C — Documents that Establish Employment Eligibility

1. U.S. social security card issued by the Social Security Administration *(other than a card stating it is not valid for employment)*

2. Certification of Birth Abroad issued by the Department of State *(Form FS-545 or Form DS-1350)*

3. Original or certified copy of a birth certificate issued by a state, county, municipal authority or outlying possession of the United States bearing an official seal

4. Native American tribal document

5. U.S. Citizen ID Card *(INS Form I-197)*

6. ID Card for use of Resident Citizen in the United States *(INS Form I-179)*

7. Unexpired employment authorization document issued by the INS *(other then those listed under List A)*

Illustrations of many of these documents appear in Part 8 of the Handbook for Employers (M-274)

Among other things, Form I-9 requires the employer to attest that it has reviewed documentation provided by the employee to establish his or her eligibility and that the documentation appears genuine. The employee must also attest to his or her eligibility to work in the U.S. USCIS has several other helpful publications, including a *Handbook for Employers* and various information bulletins. The following websites can provide more information:

http://uscis.gov/graphics/lawsregs/handbook/hand_emp.pdf

http://uscis.gov/graphics/services/employerinfo/eibulletin.htm

There are a variety of documents that can establish eligibility to work. However, it is *up to the candidate* to choose which documents (among those listed on Form I-9) to show the employer. The employer cannot specify the documents it wishes to see. If the exhibited document or documents appear to be genuine, eligibility to work is established. Form I-9 should then be completed and kept on file for at least one year after the employee leaves, but not less than three years after the employment began.

It is good practice, though not required, to make a photocopy of any documents exhibited by the employee to establish his or her eligibility to work. However, attaching a photocopy of an exhibited document is *not* a substitute for filling out Form I-9 completely.

The verification process must be completed within three working days after the employee begins work. (For employees who are hired for three days or fewer, the entire verification process must be completed on the first day of employment.) For employees whose eligibility to work here is only temporary, the employer must either reverify eligibility or terminate the employee upon expiration of the initial eligibility period.

In addition to criminal exposure, employers who fail to comply with I-9 requirements face civil liability. Several courts have ruled that an employer who uses illegal aliens can be sued by competitors under the federal *Racketeer Influenced and Corrupt Organizations Act* (RICO).

New Hire Reports

Federal law requires each state to establish a *Directory of New Hires* database. The database is then shared with other states to track persons who have child support obligations. The information is also used to detect fraud or abuse in welfare and unemployment programs. (A detailed description of the program is available from the Administration for Children and Families of the U.S. Department of Health and Human Services at **www.acf.hhs.gov/programs/cse/newhire/employer/private/nh/newhire.htm**.)

The states, in turn, have passed laws to establish the Directory and to require in-state employers to report new hires within twenty days after hiring. The one-page form can be mailed or faxed. Forms can be obtained—and in some cases, completed—online. A complete listing of state new hire agencies is in Appendix C. (Check for updated information at **www.acf.hhs.gov/programs/cse/newhire/employer/contacts/contacts.htm**.)

Multistate employers (employers with employees in more than one state) have two reporting options. They can report each newly hired employee to the state where the employee is working, following the new hire reporting regulations of that particular state, or they can select one state where they have employees working and report all new hires to that state electronically. Employers must choose between the two options—they cannot use both. Employers who choose the second option must register with the U.S. Department of Health and Human Services as a multistate employer. More information on multistate reporting and the multistate registration form are available from the Department of Health and Human Services. Contact them at:

Department of Health and Human Services
Administration for Children and Families
Office of Child Support Enforcement Multistate Employer Notification
P.O. Box 509
Randallstown, MD 21133
410-277-9470

Tax Withholding

When an employee is initially hired and whenever the employee's tax withholdings need to be changed, the employee must submit IRS Form W-4 to his or her employer. Form W-4 calls for basic information such as the employee's name, address, Social Security number, and marital status. It also contains a worksheet for figuring the number of exemptions to be claimed on the employee's tax return and various other factors that affect the employee's tax liability. These factors, known as *allowances*, are then totaled and entered on the form. Finally, Form W-4 permits the employee to claim a complete exemption from federal income tax withholding under certain conditions.

When a Form W-4 claims more than ten withholding allowances or claims an exemption from withholding that would otherwise amount to more than $200 per week, a copy must be submitted to the IRS. The IRS may then direct the employer to withhold on some different basis. (Questions about withholding obligations are spelled out in *Circular E, Employer's Tax Guide* (also known as *Publication 15*), available at **www.irs.gov**.)

Most states have their own equivalent to Form W-4. The state form needs to be completed as part of the employer's state income tax withholding requirement. (A sample of the current Form W-4 follows this section.)

Form W-4 (2004)

Purpose. Complete Form W-4 so that your employer can withhold the correct Federal income tax from your pay. Because your tax situation may change, you may want to refigure your withholding each year.

Exemption from withholding. If you are exempt, complete only lines 1, 2, 3, 4, and 7 and sign the form to validate it. Your exemption for 2004 expires February 16, 2005. See **Pub. 505,** Tax Withholding and Estimated Tax.

Note: You cannot claim exemption from withholding if: **(a)** your income exceeds $800 and includes more than $250 of unearned income (e.g., interest and dividends) and **(b)** another person can claim you as a dependent on their tax return.

Basic instructions. If you are not exempt, complete the **Personal Allowances Worksheet** below. The worksheets on page 2 adjust your withholding allowances based on itemized deductions, certain credits, adjustments to income, or two-earner/two-job situations. Complete all worksheets that apply. **However, you may claim fewer (or zero) allowances.**

Head of household. Generally, you may claim head of household filing status on your tax return only if you are unmarried and pay more than 50% of the costs of keeping up a home for yourself and your dependent(s) or other qualifying individuals. See line E below.

Tax credits. You can take projected tax credits into account in figuring your allowable number of withholding allowances. Credits for child or dependent care expenses and the child tax credit may be claimed using the **Personal Allowances Worksheet** below. See **Pub. 919,** How Do I Adjust My Tax Withholding? for information on converting your other credits into withholding allowances.

Nonwage income. If you have a large amount of nonwage income, such as interest or dividends, consider making estimated tax payments using **Form 1040-ES,** Estimated Tax for Individuals. Otherwise, you may owe additional tax.

Two earners/two jobs. If you have a working spouse or more than one job, figure the total number of allowances you are entitled to claim on all jobs using worksheets from only one Form W-4. Your withholding usually will be most accurate when all allowances are claimed on the Form W-4 for the highest paying job and zero allowances are claimed on the others.

Nonresident alien. If you are a nonresident alien, see the **Instructions for Form 8233** before completing this Form W-4.

Check your withholding. After your Form W-4 takes effect, use Pub. 919 to see how the dollar amount you are having withheld compares to your projected total tax for 2004. See Pub. 919, especially if your earnings exceed $125,000 (Single) or $175,000 (Married).

Recent name change? If your name on line 1 differs from that shown on your social security card, call 1-800-772-1213 to initiate a name change and obtain a social security card showing your correct name.

Personal Allowances Worksheet (Keep for your records.)

A Enter "1" for **yourself** if no one else can claim you as a dependent . . . . **A** _____

B Enter "1" if:
- You are single and have only one job; or
- You are married, have only one job, and your spouse does not work; or
- Your wages from a second job or your spouse's wages (or the total of both) are $1,000 or less.
. . **B** _____

C Enter "1" for your **spouse.** But, you may choose to enter "-0-" if you are married and have either a working spouse or more than one job. (Entering "-0-" may help you avoid having too little tax withheld.) . . . . **C** _____

D Enter number of **dependents** (other than your spouse or yourself) you will claim on your tax return . . . . . **D** _____

E Enter "1" if you will file as **head of household** on your tax return (see conditions under **Head of household** above) . **E** _____

F Enter "1" if you have at least $1,500 of **child or dependent care expenses** for which you plan to claim a credit . . **F** _____

(**Note:** Do **not** include child support payments. See Pub. 503, Child and Dependent Care Expenses, for details.)

G **Child Tax Credit** (including additional child tax credit):
- If your total income will be less than $52,000 ($77,000 if married), enter "2" for each eligible child.
- If your total income will be between $52,000 and $84,000 ($77,000 and $119,000 if married), enter "1" for each eligible child plus "1" **additional** if you have four or more eligible children. . . . . **G** _____

H Add lines A through G and enter total here. **Note:** This may be different from the number of exemptions you claim on your tax return. ► **H** _____

For accuracy, complete all worksheets that apply.
- If you plan to **itemize or claim adjustments to income** and want to reduce your withholding, see the **Deductions and Adjustments Worksheet** on page 2.
- If you have **more than one job** or are **married and you and your spouse both work** and the combined earnings from all jobs exceed $35,000 ($25,000 if married) see the **Two-Earner/Two-Job Worksheet** on page 2 to avoid having too little tax withheld.
- If **neither** of the above situations applies, **stop here** and enter the number from line H on line 5 of Form W-4 below.

· · · · · · · · · · Cut here and give Form W-4 to your employer. Keep the top part for your records. · · · · · · · · · ·

Form **W-4**

Department of the Treasury
Internal Revenue Service

Employee's Withholding Allowance Certificate

► Your employer must send a copy of this form to the IRS if: (a) you claim more than 10 allowances or (b) you claim "Exempt" and your wages are normally more than $200 per week.

OMB No. 1545-0010

2004

1 Type or print your first name and middle initial	Last name		2 Your social security number

Home address (number and street or rural route)

3 ☐ Single ☐ Married ☐ Married, but withhold at higher Single rate.
Note: If married, but legally separated, or spouse is a nonresident alien, check the "Single" box.

City or town, state, and ZIP code

4 If your last name differs from that shown on your social security card, check here. You must call 1-800-772-1213 for a new card. ► ☐

5 Total number of allowances you are claiming (from line **H** above **or** from the applicable worksheet on page 2) **5** _____

6 Additional amount, if any, you want withheld from each paycheck . . . . **6** $_____

7 I claim exemption from withholding for 2004, and I certify that I meet **both** of the following conditions for exemption:
- Last year I had a right to a refund of **all** Federal income tax withheld because I had **no** tax liability **and**
- This year I expect a refund of **all** Federal income tax withheld because I expect to have **no** tax liability.

If you meet both conditions, write "Exempt" here . . . . ► **7** _____

Under penalties of perjury, I certify that I am entitled to the number of withholding allowances claimed on this certificate, or I am entitled to claim exempt status.

Employee's signature
(Form is not valid
unless you sign it.) ►

Date ►

8 Employer's name and address (Employer: Complete lines 8 and 10 only if sending to the IRS.)	9 Office code (optional)	10 Employer identification number (EIN)

For Privacy Act and Paperwork Reduction Act Notice, see page 2. Cat. No. 10220Q Form **W-4** (2004)

Form W-4 (2004)   Page **2**

Deductions and Adjustments Worksheet

Note: *Use this worksheet **only** if you plan to itemize deductions, claim certain credits, or claim adjustments to income on your 2004 tax return.*

1 Enter an estimate of your 2004 itemized deductions. These include qualifying home mortgage interest, charitable contributions, state and local taxes, medical expenses in excess of 7.5% of your income, and miscellaneous deductions. (For 2004, you may have to reduce your itemized deductions if your income is over $142,700 ($71,350 if married filing separately). See **Worksheet 3** in Pub. 919 for details.) . . . .   **1** $ _____

2 Enter:
$9,700 if married filing jointly or qualifying widow(er)
$7,150 if head of household
$4,850 if single
$4,850 if married filing separately . . . .   **2** $ _____

3 **Subtract** line 2 from line 1. If line 2 is greater than line 1, enter "-0-" . . . .   **3** $ _____

4 Enter an estimate of your 2004 adjustments to income, including alimony, deductible IRA contributions, and student loan interest   **4** $ _____

5 **Add** lines 3 and 4 and enter the total. (Include any amount for credits from **Worksheet 7** in Pub. 919) ..   **5** $ _____

6 Enter an estimate of your 2004 nonwage income (such as dividends or interest) . . . .   **6** $ _____

7 **Subtract** line 6 from line 5. Enter the result, but not less than "-0-" . . . .   **7** $ _____

8 **Divide** the amount on line 7 by $3,000 and enter the result here. Drop any fraction . . . . .   **8** _____

9 Enter the number from the **Personal Allowances Worksheet,** line H, page 1 . . . .   **9** _____

10 **Add** lines 8 and 9 and enter the total here. If you plan to use the **Two-Earner/Two-Job Worksheet,** also enter this total on line 1 below. Otherwise, **stop here** and enter this total on Form W-4, line 5, page 1 ..   **10** _____

Two-Earner/Two-Job Worksheet (See Two earners/two jobs on page 1.)

Note: *Use this worksheet **only** if the instructions under line H on page 1 direct you here.*

1 Enter the number from line 1, page 1 (or from line 10 above if you used the **Deductions and Adjustments Worksheet**)   **1** _____

2 Find the number in **Table 1** below that applies to the **LOWEST** paying job and enter it here . . . .   **2** _____

3 If line 1 is **more than or equal to** line 2, subtract line 2 from line 1. Enter the result here (if zero, enter "-0-") and on Form W-4, line 5, page 1. **Do not** use the rest of this worksheet . . . .   **3** _____

Note: *If line 1 is **less than** line 2, enter "-0-" on Form W-4, line 5, page 1. Complete lines 4-9 below to calculate the additional withholding amount necessary to avoid a year-end tax bill.*

4 Enter the number from line 2 of this worksheet . . . .   **4** _____

5 Enter the number from line 1 of this worksheet . . . .   **5** _____

6 **Subtract** line 5 from line 4 . . . .   **6** _____

7 Find the amount in **Table 2** below that applies to the **HIGHEST** paying job and enter it here . . . ..   **7** $ _____

8 **Multiply** line 7 by line 6 and enter the result here. This is the additional annual withholding needed . ..   **8** $ _____

9 Divide line 8 by the number of pay periods remaining in 2004. For example, divide by 26 if you are paid every two weeks and you complete this form in December 2003. Enter the result here and on Form W-4, line 6, page 1. This is the additional amount to be withheld from each paycheck . . . .   **9** $ _____

Table 1: Two-Earner/Two-Job Worksheet

Married Filing Jointly			**Married Filing Jointly**			**All Others**	
If wages from **HIGHEST** paying job are-	AND, wages from **LOWEST** paying job are-	Enter on line 2 above	If wages from **HIGHEST** paying job are-	AND, wages from **LOWEST** paying job are-	Enter on line 2 above	If wages from **LOWEST** paying job are-	Enter on line 2 above
$0 - $40,000	$0 - $4,000	0	$40,001 and over	31,001 - 38,000	6	$0 - $6,000	0
	4,001 - 8,000	1		38,001 - 44,000	7	6,001 - 11,000	1
	8,001 - 17,000	2		44,001 - 50,000	8	11,001 - 18,000	2
	17,001 and over	3		50,001 - 55,000	9	18,001 - 25,000	3
$40,001 and over	$0 - $4,000	0		55,001 - 65,000	10	25,001 - 31,000	4
	4,001 - 8,000	1		65,001 - 75,000	11	31,001 - 44,000	5
	8,001 - 15,000	2		75,001 - 85,000	12	44,001 - 55,000	6
	15,001 - 22,000	3		85,001 - 100,000	13	55,001 - 70,000	7
	22,001 - 25,000	4		100,001 - 115,000	14	70,001 - 80,000	8
	25,001 - 31,000	5		115,001 and over	15	80,001 - 100,000	9
						100,001 and over	10

Table 2: Two-Earner/Two-Job Worksheet

Married Filing Jointly		**All Others**	
If wages from **HIGHEST** paying job are-	Enter on line 7 above	If wages from **HIGHEST** paying job are-	Enter on line 7 above
$0 - $60,000	$470	$0 - $30,000	$470
60,001 - 110,000	780	30,001 - 70,000	780
110,001 - 150,000	870	70,001 - 140,000	870
150,001 - 270,000	1,020	140,001 - 320,000	1,020
270,001 and over	1,090	320,001 and over	1,090

Earned Income Credit

The *earned income credit* (EIC) is normally a matter just between the employee and the IRS. However, when an employee expects to be in a negative tax situation at the end of the year, he or she may notify the employer of that fact using Form W-5, and the employer then is obligated to advance the negative tax in the employee's pay checks. Only employees with one or more dependent children are eligible for advances. The IRS's Circular E contains tables for determining the amount to be included in each pay check. The employer is reimbursed for the advances by claiming them as a credit on the employer's withholding tax deposits. (A sample Form W-5 follows on the next three pages.)

2004 Form W-5

Department of the Treasury
Internal Revenue Service

Instructions

Purpose of Form

Use Form W-5 if you are eligible to get part of the EIC in advance with your pay and choose to do so. See **Who Is Eligible To Get Advance EIC Payments?** below. The amount you can get in advance generally depends on your wages. If you are married, the amount of your advance EIC payments also depends on whether your spouse has filed a Form W-5 with his or her employer. However, your employer cannot give you more than $1,563 throughout 2004 with your pay. You will get the rest of any EIC you are entitled to when you file your tax return and claim the EIC.

If you do not choose to get advance payments, you can still claim the EIC on your 2004 tax return.

What Is the EIC?

The EIC is a credit for certain workers. It reduces the tax you owe. It may give you a refund even if you do not owe any tax.

Who Is Eligible To Get Advance EIC Payments?

You are eligible to get advance EIC payments if **all three** of the following apply.

1. You expect to have at least one qualifying child. If you do not expect to have a qualifying child, you may still be eligible for the EIC, but you **cannot** receive advance EIC payments. See **Who Is a Qualifying Child?** below.

2. You expect that your 2004 earned income and AGI will each be less than $30,338 ($31,338 if you expect to file a joint return for 2004). Include your spouse's income if you plan to file a joint return. As used on this form, **earned income** does not include amounts inmates in

penal institutions are paid for their work, amounts received as a pension or annuity from a nonqualified deferred compensation plan or a nongovernmental section 457 plan, or nontaxable earned income.

3. You expect to be able to claim the EIC for 2004. To find out if you may be able to claim the EIC, answer the questions on page 2.

How To Get Advance EIC Payments

If you are eligible to get advance EIC payments, fill in the 2004 Form W-5 at the bottom of this page. Then, detach it and give it to your employer. If you get advance payments, you **must** file a 2004 Federal income tax return.

You may have only **one** Form W-5 in effect at one time. If you and your spouse are both employed, you should file separate Forms W-5.

This Form W-5 expires on December 31, 2004. If you are eligible to get advance EIC payments for 2005, you must file a new Form W-5 next year.

TIP You may be able to get a larger credit when you file your 2004 return. For details, see **Additional Credit** on page 3.

Who Is a Qualifying Child?

Any child who meets **all three** of the following conditions is a **qualifying child.**

1. The child is:

● Your son, daughter, adopted child, stepchild, or a descendant of any of them (for example, your grandchild); or

● Your brother, sister, stepbrother, stepsister, or a descendant of any of them (for example, your niece or nephew), whom you cared for as you would your own child; or

● A foster child (any child placed with you by an authorized placement agency whom you cared for as you would your own child).

(continued on page 3)

▼ *Give the bottom part to your employer; keep the top part for your records.* ▼

-- Detach here --

Form **W-5**

Department of the Treasury
Internal Revenue Service

Earned Income Credit Advance Payment Certificate

▶ Use the current year's certificate only.
▶ Give this certificate to your employer.
▶ This certificate expires on December 31, 2004.

OMB No. 1545-1342

2004

Print or type your full name	Your social security number
	: :

Note: *If you get advance payments of the earned income credit for 2004, you **must** file a 2004 Federal income tax return. To get advance payments, you **must** have a qualifying child and your filing status must be any status **except** married filing a separate return.*

1 I expect to have a qualifying child and be able to claim the earned income credit for 2004, I do not have another Form W-5 in effect with any other current employer, and I choose to get advance EIC payments . . ☐ **Yes** ☐ **No**

2 Check the box that shows your expected filing status for 2004:
☐ Single, head of household, or qualifying widow(er) ☐ Married filing jointly

3 If you are married, does your spouse have a Form W-5 in effect for 2004 with any employer? . . . . . . ☐ **Yes** ☐ **No**

Under penalties of perjury, I declare that the information I have furnished above is, to the best of my knowledge, true, correct, and complete.

Signature ▶   Date ▶

Cat. No. 10227P

Questions To See if You May Be Able To Claim the EIC for 2004

⚠️ **CAUTION** You **cannot** claim the EIC if you plan to file either **Form 2555** or **Form 2555-EZ** (relating to foreign earned income) for 2004. You also **cannot** claim the EIC if you are a nonresident alien for any part of 2004 unless you are married to a U.S. citizen or resident, file a joint return, and elect to be taxed as a resident alien for all of 2004.

1 Do you expect to have a qualifying child? Read **Who Is a Qualifying Child?** that starts on page 1 before you answer this question. If the child is married, be sure you also read **Married child** on page 3.

☐ **No.** (STOP) You may be able to claim the EIC but you **cannot** get advance EIC payments.
☐ **Yes.** *Continue.*

⚠️ **CAUTION** If the child meets the conditions to be a qualifying child for both you and another person, see **Qualifying child of more than one person** on page 3.

2 Do you expect your 2004 filing status to be married filing a separate return?

☐ **Yes.** (STOP) You **cannot** claim the EIC.
☐ **No.** *Continue.*

💡 **TIP** If you expect to file a joint return for 2004, include your spouse's income when answering questions 3 and 4.

3 Do you expect that your 2004 earned income and AGI will each be less than: $30,338 ($31,338 if married filing jointly) if you expect to have 1 qualifying child; $34,458 ($35,458 if married filing jointly) if you expect to have 2 or more qualifying children?

☐ **No.** (STOP) You **cannot** claim the EIC.
☐ **Yes.** *Continue.* But remember, you **cannot** get advance EIC payments if you expect your 2004 earned income or AGI will be $30,338 ($31,338 or more if married filing jointly) or more.

4 Do you expect that your 2004 investment income will be more than $2,650? For most people, investment income is the total of their taxable interest, ordinary dividends, capital gain distributions, and tax-exempt interest. However, if you plan to file a 2004 Form 1040, see the 2003 Form 1040 instructions to figure your investment income.

☐ **Yes.** (STOP) You **cannot** claim the EIC.
☐ **No.** *Continue.*

5 Do you expect that you, or your spouse if filing a joint return, will be a qualifying child of another person for 2004?
☐ **No.** You may be able to claim the EIC.
☐ **Yes.** You **cannot** claim the EIC.

Note: *An adopted child is always treated as your own child. An adopted child includes a child placed with you by an authorized placement agency for legal adoption even if the adoption is not final. An authorized placement agency includes any person or court authorized by state law to place children for legal adoption.*

2. At the end of 2004, the child is under age 19, or under age 24 and a full-time student, or any age and permanently and totally disabled.

3. The child lives with you in the United States for over half of 2004.

Exception to "Time Lived With You" Condition. The child does not have to live with you for over half of 2004 if either of the following applies.

1. The child was born or died during the year and your home was this child's home for the entire time he or she was alive in 2004.

2. The child is presumed by law enforcement authorities to have been kidnapped by someone who is not a family member and the child lived with you for over half of the part of the year before he or she was kidnapped.

Note: *Temporary absences, such as for school, vacation, medical care, or detention in a juvenile facility, count as time lived at home. Members of the military on extended active duty outside the United States are considered to be living in the United States.*

Married child. A child who is married at the end of 2004 is a qualifying child only if you may claim him or her as your dependent, **or** the following **Exception** applies to you.

Exception. You are the custodial parent and would be able to claim the child as your dependent, but the noncustodial parent claims the child as a dependent because–

1. You signed **Form 8332,** Release of Claim to Exemption for Child of Divorced or Separated Parents, or a similar statement, agreeing not to claim the child for 2004 **or**

2. You have a pre-1985 divorce decree or separation agreement that allows the noncustodial parent to claim the child and he or she gives at least $600 for the child's support in 2004.

Other rules may apply. See **Pub. 501,** Exemptions, Standard Deduction, and Filing Information, for more information on children of divorced or separated parents.

Qualifying child of more than one person. If the child meets the conditions to be a qualifying child of more than one person, only one person may treat that child as a qualifying child for 2004. If you and the other person(s) cannot agree on who will treat that child as a qualifying child for 2004, special rules apply to determine who may do so. For details, see the 2003 revision of **Pub. 596,** Earned Income Credit (EIC). However, these rules do not apply if the only other person is your spouse and you plan to file a joint return for 2004.

Reminder. A qualifying child must have a social security number unless he or she was born and died in 2004.

What if My Situation Changes?

If your situation changes after you give Form W-5 to your employer, you will probably need to file a new Form W-5. For example, you must file a new Form W-5 if any of the following applies for 2004.

● You no longer expect to have a qualifying child. Check **"No"** on line 1 of your new Form W-5.

● You no longer expect to be able to claim the EIC for 2004. Check **"No"** on line 1 of your new Form W-5.

● You no longer want advance payments. Check **"No"** on line 1 of your new Form W-5.

● Your spouse files Form W-5 with his or her employer. Check **"Yes"** on line 3 of your new Form W-5.

Note: *If you get the EIC with your pay and find you are not eligible, you must pay it back when you file your 2004 Federal income tax return.*

Additional Information

How To Claim the EIC

If you are eligible, claim the EIC on your 2004 tax return. See your 2004 tax return instruction booklet.

Additional Credit

You may be able to claim a larger credit when you file your 2004 Form 1040 or Form 1040A because your employer cannot give you more than $1,563 throughout the year with your pay. You may also be able to claim a larger credit if you have more than one qualifying child. But you must file your 2004 tax return to claim any additional credit.

Privacy Act and Paperwork Reduction Act Notice. We ask for the information on this form to carry out the Internal Revenue laws of the United States. Internal Revenue Code sections 3507 and 6109 and their regulations require you to provide the information requested on Form W-5 and to give it to your employer if you want advance payment of the EIC. As provided by law, we may give the information to the Department of Justice and other Federal agencies. In addition, we may give it to cities, states, and the District of Columbia so they may carry out their tax laws. We may also disclose this information to other countries under a tax treaty or to Federal and state agencies to enforce Federal nontax criminal laws and to combat terrorism. Failure to provide the requested information may prevent your employer from processing this form; providing false information may subject you to penalties.

You are not required to provide the information requested on a form that is subject to the Paperwork Reduction Act unless the form displays a valid OMB control number. Books or records relating to a form or its instructions must be retained as long as their contents may become material in the administration of any Internal Revenue law. Generally, tax returns and return information are confidential, as required by Code section 6103.

The time needed to complete this form will vary depending on individual circumstances. The estimated average time is: **Recordkeeping,** 6 min.; **Learning about the law or the form,** 12 min.; and **Preparing the form,** 25 min.

We welcome comments on forms. If you have comments concerning the accuracy of these time estimates or suggestions for making this form simpler, we would be happy to hear from you. You can write to the Tax Products Coordinating Committee, Western Area Distribution Center, Rancho Cordova, CA 95743-0001. **Do not** send Form W-5 to this address. Instead, give it to your employer.

Statutory Employees and Non-Employees

For tax withholding purposes, the IRS classifies the following workers as employees (called *statutory employees*), even if they might otherwise be considered independent contractors:

- an agent (or commission) driver who delivers food, beverages (other than milk), laundry, or dry cleaning for someone else;
- a full-time life, insurance salesperson who sells primarily for one company;
- a homeworker who works by guidelines of the person for whom the work is done, with materials furnished by and returned to that person or to someone that person designates; and,
- a traveling or city salesperson (other than an agent driver or commission driver) who works full time (except for sideline sales activities) for one firm getting orders from customers. The orders must be for items for resale or use as supplies in the customer's business. The customers must be retailers, wholesalers, contractors, or operators of hotels, restaurants, or other businesses dealing with food or lodging.

In contrast, the IRS classifies *direct sellers* and *licensed real estate agents* as independent contractors (called *statutory non-employees*), even though they might otherwise be considered employees. *Direct sellers* include persons engaged in selling consumer products in the home or place of business other than in a permanent retail establishment.

In order for direct sellers and licensed real estate agents to qualify for statutory, non-employee classification both of the following must be true.

1. Substantially all their compensation must be directly related to sales or other output, rather than to the number of hours worked.

2. Their services must be performed under a written contract providing that they will not be treated as employees for federal tax purposes.

Social Security Number Verification

Each new employee must have a valid Social Security number (SSN) that matches his or her name. The Social Security Administration has established a voluntary *Employee Verification Service* to verify matches and report mismatches. (The service is explained at **www.ssa.gov/employer/ssnv.htm**.)

The service is also covered in a brochure available at the same website.

Example

A new employee of a Minnesota autobody shop refused to provide a Social Security number (SSN) at hiring time, claiming that he did not use an SSN because it represented the mark of the beast as described in the Christian Bible's Book of Revelation. When the autobody shop rejected him for employment, he sued for religious discrimination, arguing that the employer had a duty to reasonably accommodate his religious beliefs. A federal appeals court sided with the autobody shop, saying that providing an SSN was an IRS—not an employer—requirement. Further, forcing an employer to violate the Internal Revenue Code and subject itself to potential penalties by not providing an employee's SSN on tax reports would not be a reasonable accommodation, but would instead amount to an undue hardship. Even expecting an employer to apply to the IRS for a waiver of the SSN requirement would be unreasonable.

Seaworth v. Pearson, 203 F.3d 1056 (8th Cir. 2000)

Suppose an employer obtains Form W-4 from its employee and then, at year's end, issues a W-2 to the employee showing taxable income paid during the year and sends a copy of the W-2 to the Social Security Administration, all as required by law. Sometime later, the employer gets a *no-match notice* from the Administration stating that, according to the Administration's records, the employee's name and SSN do not match. How should the employer respond? Should the employer assume that the employee gave a fake Social Security number on his or her W-4? Should the employer fire the employee on the assumption that the employee is an illegal alien?

Firing the employee solely on the basis of a no-match notice could be risky. The same federal law that prohibits the employment of undocumented workers also prohibits discrimination on the basis of citizenship status or national origin. The mismatch could be the result of an employer error in recording the employee's SSN on the W-2, the result of an employee name change through marriage or divorce, or the result of an error on the employee's W-4. So any adverse action taken on the strength of a no-match notice could amount to illegal discrimination.

Instead, on receipt of a no-match letter, the employer should:

- check the employer's own records for errors;
- provide a copy of the no-match notice to the employee and ask the employee to check his or her records;
- promptly report any corrected information to the Social Security Administration; and,
- if no obvious errors in the employer's or employee's records are apparent, suggest that the employee contact the Social Security Administration for help.

Example

The Social Security Administration notified a manufacturing company in Illinois that a number of the W-2s the company had filed contained name/SSN mismatches. The company's human resources administrator investigated, but finding no error in the company's own

(continued)

records, concluded that the employees were undocumented aliens and recommended that the employees be fired. Before acting on the administrator's recommendation, the company checked with the Social Security Administration and with its attorney and, with that advice, decided to send letters to each of the employees asking them to correct any errors.

Believing that approach to be unlawful, the administrator refused to process the new information submitted by the employees and she was fired for insubordination. The administrator then sued, claiming that her firing was in retaliation for attempting to comply with federal immigration laws and that the firing was abusive under Illinois law. A federal appeals court rejected the administrator's claims, noting that the company did exactly what the Social Security Administration and its own legal counsel had suggested.

Arres v. IMI Cornelius Remcor, Inc., 333 F.3d 812 (7th Cir. 2003)

Benefit Plan Participation

New employees may be eligible immediately or after a brief waiting period to enroll in any group benefit plans you provide, such as medical expense insurance coverage, life insurance, disability insurance, cafeteria plans, etc. Retirement plans often have a somewhat longer waiting period—anywhere from six months to as long as two years. It is important to track these waiting periods to be sure that employees are enrolled as soon as they become eligible or are at least offered the option of enrolling. Failure to enroll eligible employees could amount to a breach of contract with the insurance company that underwrites the plan, it could expose you to suit by the employees, and it could even jeopardize the favorable tax status of the plan itself.

> **Example**
>
> A multinational software manufacturer classified a number of its workers as independent contractors and did not offer fringe benefits to them or withhold taxes from them. Many of these workers had been at their same jobs for years, working on teams along with regular employees, reporting to the same supervisors, performing identical functions, and working the same core hours. After the IRS reclassified the workers as employees, the workers sued the company for benefits they claimed should have been extended to them. In what became known as the *perma-temp case*, the company eventually agreed to a settlement of the workers' claims of almost $97 million.
>
> *Vizcaino v. Microsoft Corp.*, 290 F.3d 1043 (9th Cir. 2002)

Training

For the most part, any training a new employee gets—either formal or on-the-job—will be dictated purely by business considerations. Two training topics, however, go beyond business considerations and implicate legal issues—*discrimination* and *safety and health.*

More and more courts are concluding that companies must include a training component in their discrimination policy in order for the policy to be considered effective. This is especially true in cases of sexual harassment, where having an effective policy is a critical element of an employer's defense to harassment claims.

> **Example**
>
> A guard at a county jail in New Jersey brought suit against the county under New Jersey's discrimination law, claiming that her supervisor harassed her by forcibly kissing her on one occasion. The supervisor
>
> *(continued)*

also brought up the kissing incident a number of times in front of other employees and he even threatened to rape her. Although the guard had told co-workers about the original kissing incident, she never filed a formal complaint with the county. The county responded to the lawsuit saying that it had an anti-harassment policy in place, which the guard failed to take advantage of. Therefore, according to the county, it should not be liable. The New Jersey Supreme Court allowed the guard's suit to proceed, pointing to evidence that despite the existence of an anti-harassment policy, the county failed to train any of its employees concerning the policy. The absence of training, said the court, could support the conclusion that the county did not have an *effective* and *realistic* anti-harassment policy and that the policy was one in name only.

Gaines v. Bellino, 801 A.2d 322 (N.J. 2002)

In the safety and health area, the Occupational Safety and Health Administration (OSHA) requires safety training for a number of hazardous occupations. Under the heading "Safety Training and Education," an OSHA regulation requires employers to *instruct each employee in the recognition and avoidance of unsafe conditions and the regulations applicable to his work environment to control or eliminate any hazards or other exposure to illness or injury.* Violation of OSHA regulations can result in substantial civil penalties and intentional violations can result in criminal convictions.

Part II

Firing

14

The Decision-Making Process

Firing an employee is almost as difficult as being fired. It is a bit like going to a funeral—while most of us would prefer to be mourners than to be the one mourned, the event cannot help but remind us of our own vulnerability.

From the employee's perspective, getting fired is likely to produce denial, anger, resentment, and a desire for revenge. In some cases, this can lead to violence. In other cases, it leads to a lawsuit. The decision to fire should not be made lightly.

Grounds for Termination

When you find yourself tempted to fire an employee, the question you must first ask yourself is "*Do I have good, business-related grounds to take this action?*" Although in states recognizing the doctrine of at-will employment you can fire an at-will employee for any reason (except an illegal reason) or for no reason at all, *it never makes sense to do so.* When an employer exercises its business judgment in terminating an at-will employee, courts have no right to substitute their own views in the matter or ask themselves whether they would have fired the employee in the same circumstances. But if the employer cannot identify and articulate a business-related reason for the termination, such as poor performance, serious misconduct, or repeated misconduct, the employee involved (and the jury) will likely assume that the firing was for a discriminatory or other illegal reason.

Need for Documentation

Employers must *document* the problem that gave rise to the termination. If the problem was poor performance, the employer should be able to point to tasks listed in a job description that were not performed satisfactorily. If the problem related to misconduct, then the behavioral standard that the employee failed to meet should be contained in the employee handbook. The instances of poor performance or misconduct that gave rise to the termination should also be noted in writing in the employee's personnel file and on periodic evaluations. Jurors simply will not believe that a performance or behavioral issue was significant enough to justify termination if at the same time it was too insignificant to be noted in the employee's personnel file.

Progressive Discipline

Progressive discipline can play an important role here. If the problem has repeatedly been brought to the employee's attention, with appropriate notations made in his or her personnel file, then the final blow—termination—should not come as a big surprise and the employee is less likely to claim illegality. Should the employee nevertheless decide to sue, a jury—when told of a recurring, documented performance or behavioral issue—is much less likely to ascribe an illegal motive to the employer.

For less serious offenses, a progressive discipline policy might typically include the following steps:

- oral warning;
- written warning;
- suspension without pay;
- demotion; and,
- termination.

Offenses meriting a multi-step approach might include tardiness, excessive absenteeism, minor neglect of work, and frequent personal phone calls.

The employee handbook should not promise that a progressive disciplinary procedure will be followed. There are times when a behavioral or performance issue is just too serious to allow the employment relationship to continue unaltered. More serious offenses justifying immediate suspension, demotion, or termination might include:

- insubordination;
- theft or unauthorized use of company property or property of fellow employees;
- use or possession of illegal substances or weapons;
- other illegal activity, such as gambling on company premises or use of company facilities to transmit obscene material;
- violence or threats of violence against supervisors;
- racial or sexual harassment;
- intentional discrimination;
- falsifying records or reports; and,
- willful disregard of important company policies, such as workplace safety procedures.

The list is not complete. Discipline needs to be tailored to each employer's circumstances. An inventory clerk's mistake in logging in new supplies, for example, is not the equivalent of a nurse's inaccurate recording of vital signs in a patient's medical chart.

Contractual Restrictions

A decision to fire must be consistent with any applicable contractual provisions between the employer and the employee or between the employer and the employee's union. A contract may require the parties to give advance notice, such as two weeks, thirty days, or six months. In those situations, the employer is probably free to relieve the employee of all further duties immediately, but the employer will still be obligated to pay salary and benefits during the notice period.

Good Cause

The employee may have a contract that permits termination only for *good cause*. What does good cause mean in this context? The parties to the contract may already have defined the terms by listing all the events that constitutes good cause, such as:

- conviction of a felony involving dishonesty;
- engaging in a competing business; and,
- threatening supervisors or co-workers.

This makes the contract more definite, but it ties the employer's hands when misconduct occurs that the parties had not anticipated. When the parties have identified specific conduct that constitutes good cause, it is usually a good idea to include a catchall, such as:

good cause includes incompetence or any other act or omission that injures the employer's business, reputation, or goodwill, exposes the employer to liability, creates a workplace safety or health hazard, or is disruptive to the discipline and good order of the workplace

-or-

the employer, in its reasonable discretion, may determine what constitutes good cause.

Some contracts do not define the term at all. In those situations, the employment relationship itself implies certain duties on the part of the employee. These include a duty to show up for work in reasonably fit condition, a duty to have and exercise reasonable skill in performing the job, a duty of loyalty and honesty, and a duty to refrain from insubordinate and threatening behavior. A substantial breach of any of these implied duties is cause for termination.

Last Chance Contracts

When an employee falls short of company expectations or requirements in some significant way, but is otherwise highly valued, the company might consider a *last chance contract* as a way of retaining the employee and encouraging him or her to resolve the shortcoming. Last chance contracts may be particularly useful in cases of substance abuse or emotional disorders that are responsive to treatment or counseling.

Example

Ira had worked at a company in Minnesota for more than twenty-six years prior to being discharged. During that time, he had recurring substance abuse battles. When the company learned about Ira's problem, it agreed that if he successfully completed treatment, he could retain his job. Ira did complete a treatment program, but after returning to work, he relapsed and entered another program. This pattern of return to work, relapse, treatment, and return to work repeated itself several times. Finally, the company entered into a last chance contract with Ira, requiring him to complete a two and one-half month program and refrain from all drug and alcohol use. Ira was subject to immediate termination if he violated any terms of the last chance contract.

Four years later, while absent from work because of a workers' compensation injury, Ira was arrested for driving while intoxicated. When the DWI came to the company's attention, the company fired him per the terms of the last chance contract. In Ira's subsequent suit under the *Americans with Disabilities Act*, a federal appeals court ruled that the

(continued)

> company's basis for terminating Ira—that he had violated the terms of his last chance contract—constituted a legitimate, nondiscriminatory reason for taking an adverse employment action. The court pointed out that Ira had voluntarily entered into the contract to preserve his job and that his violation of the contract provided justification for termination.
>
> *Longen v. Waterous Co., 347 F.3d 685 (8th Cir. 2003)*

Termination Procedure

Another important employer safeguard when terminating an employee is establishing and following a formalized procedure. The elements of such a process should include the following.

- ◆ Identification of persons who are authorized to make the decision.
- ◆ A requirement that the employee's personnel file be reviewed by someone not involved in the decision, to be sure the grounds are well documented and that all required procedures have been followed.
- ◆ Circumstances under which the decision must be reviewed by house counsel and/or outside employment law counsel.
- ◆ A requirement that any litigation risks be objectively evaluated. (Is the employee in a protected leave status? Does he or she have a contract which restricts the right to fire? Is the employee protected by any whistleblower laws? Does he or she have a complaint of discrimination pending?)
- ◆ A requirement that any business risks be objectively evaluated. (Is the employee entitled to an expensive severance package? Will termination result in loss of valued customers? How will termination affect workplace morale? Can the employee be easily replaced or can his or her functions be readily assigned to others?)

Having and following an established procedure provides strong evidence that the employer acted reasonably and not rashly or arbitrarily.

> ## Example
>
> A Wyoming nursing care center had an employee handbook that required good cause for termination, without further defining the term. The center terminated one of its nurses, citing a number of performance failures and her general rudeness to patients, their families, and fellow employees. The nurse sued, claiming that the handbook created a contract of employment and that she was fired without good cause and in breach of the contract. The trial court found in favor of the nurse, but the Wyoming Supreme Court reversed and sent the case back for further consideration, saying that so long as the employer acted in good faith, the firing should be upheld. In the court's words, the question the trial court should have addressed was not whether the nurse in fact committed the acts leading to dismissal. Instead, it should have considered whether the factual basis on which the employer concluded a dischargeable act had been committed was reached honestly, after appropriate investigation, and for reasons that were not arbitrary or pretextual.
>
> *Life Care Centers of America, Inc. v. Dexter, 65 P.3d 385 (Wyo. 2003)*

Sometimes an employer will suspect an employee of misconduct without being sure that any misconduct actually occurred or that a particular employee was responsible. For example, the employer might receive a complaint of sexual harassment, but the person accused of the harassment denies any wrongdoing. Or the company might become aware that supplies or equipment are missing, but does not know who took them. In those situations, the company needs to investigate. While the conduct of investigations goes well beyond the scope of this book, a few tips should be made here. Any such investigation should be:

- *prompt*, particularly in cases of sexual harassment in which the company's response (or lack of response) to the complaint will have a major impact on the company's liability;
- *adequate*, under the circumstances;
- *fair*, in the sense that all parties—accused as well as accuser— are given reasonable opportunity to express their positions and all sources of relevant information are considered;
- *well documented*, as to who was questioned, what they said, and what documents or files were inspected; and,
- *conducted in reasonable confidence*, so as not to damage anyone's reputation before all the facts are known.

If the decision is made to use an outside investigator, the employer should be mindful that the investigator may be considered a *consumer reporting agency*, triggering obligations under the *Fair Credit Reporting Act*. (see Chapter 24.)

15

Voluntary and Involuntary Termination

It is *not* always easy to tell whether an employee quit or was fired. The distinction can be critical, however, because it may affect a range of rights and benefits, such as cashing out accrued leave, timing of final paycheck, unemployment insurance, wrongful discharge suits, COBRA, severance pay, and eligibility for rehire.

A helpful rule of thumb is to treat a work separation as voluntary if it is initiated by the employee, but if the employer initiates the process by making it clear to the employee that continued employment will not be an option past a certain date, then the separation will be considered involuntary. Using this approach, a resignation in lieu of firing will generally be considered involuntary for most purposes. However, the determination of whether a separation is voluntary or involuntary is highly fact specific. The rule of thumb is only a rough guide that may not apply in all circumstances.

Example

A secretary in a Virginia doctor's office missed a number of days from work due to the death of a grandparent and the illness of a parent. Her employer told her that it did not like her missing days and would be looking for a replacement. The secretary then turned in a resignation,

(continued)

> but agreed to stay on until a replacement was found. When a replacement was hired, the secretary applied for unemployment insurance. The secretary was denied benefits on the basis that her resignation was merely *in anticipation of* being fired, not *in lieu of* being fired.
>
> *Virginia Unemployment Comm. v. Hill, 2004 WL 941233 (Va.App. 2004)*

Despite the result in the example, employers should keep in mind that for unemployment insurance purposes, close cases are likely to be decided in favor of awarding benefits.

Should an employer allow an employee to resign in lieu of being fired? From the employer's perspective, there is probably little to be gained in doing so, since the termination will still be listed as involuntary in the employer's records and the employee will probably still be able to collect unemployment insurance and sue for wrongful discharge. Since many employers do not give substantive references anyway, it will make little difference how the separation is characterized in terms of the employer's response to inquiries from prospective employers. The only real benefit to the employer is that the separation process itself may be smoother and less confrontational.

On the other hand, allowing an employee to resign in lieu of being fired probably does no harm. In risky situations in which a lawsuit is possible, characterizing the termination as a resignation might be part of a comprehensive separation agreement that includes a release of any claims the employee might have against the employer.

Constructive Discharge

When an employer permits working conditions to become so intolerable that a reasonable person would quit, an employee who actually does quit rather than suffer the conditions may be deemed to have been fired. A voluntary separation under these circumstances is known as a *constructive discharge*.

The constructive discharge concept originated in the field of labor relations law in the 1930s. The National Labor Relations Board developed the doctrine to address situations in which employers coerced employees to resign by creating intolerable working conditions in retaliation for the employees' engaging in union activities. Since then, the concept has been expanded to cover harassment in violation of *Title VII*, safety violations, and an employer's insisting that an employee violate the law.

Tangible Employment Action

In June 2004, the U.S. Supreme Court considered a related aspect of the constructive discharge doctrine in a case called *Suders v. Pennsylvania State Police*. The employee in that case claimed that she had been sexually harassed by her supervisor to the point where she had no choice but to quit. She then sued for sex discrimination. The central issue in the case was whether the employer should be held liable for the supervisor's harassment.

In earlier cases, the Supreme Court ruled that when the harassment involves a *tangible employment action*, such as demotion or a significant change in duties, then the employer is always liable. For example, if the supervisor says "*Sleep with me and I'll promote you; don't, and I'll fire you*," the supervisor is exercising authority given by the employer and the employer is therefore liable for the misuse of that authority. However, if the harassment takes the form of a supervisor-created, sexually hostile work environment, but without any tangible employment action, then the employer may or may not be liable. In those situations, the employer has the opportunity to defend by showing that it had an effective policy against sexual harassment and that the employee unreasonably failed to take advantage of that policy.

The question in *Suders* was whether a constructive discharge is a tangible employment action (in which case the employer is always liable) or is not a tangible employment action (in which case the employer may have a defense). The Supreme Court answered that it depends on whether, in creating an intolerable working environment, the supervisor acted in his or her *official capacity* or whether the supervisor's misconduct was not aided by his or her supervisory authority and was merely similar to conduct that co-employees might commit. The Court sent the case back to the lower courts to resolve this factual issue.

Purposeful Conduct

Another question that arises is whether, in order to be considered a constructive discharge, the termination resulted from the employer's *purposeful conduct* with the intent of forcing the employee to quit. As it originally arose in the labor law field, the concept did require intentional, coercive actions by the employer. But more recent cases have applied the concept even when no intentional conduct by the employer is shown. The Supreme Court's decision in *Suders* used a definition of constructive discharge that did not include purposeful conduct by the employer.

A constructive discharge can also occur if an employee has an employment contract and, contrary to the contract, the employee's title is taken away or his or her duties are significantly diminished.

Example

The board of directors of a Massachusetts company removed the chief executive officer from his position, even though he had an employment contract, and elected another person as president. The company offered the former CEO a subsidiary position with no reduction in salary, but the former CEO rejected the offer and quit. An appeals court in Massachusetts ruled the termination a constructive discharge, saying that if an employee, especially an executive employee, is engaged to fill a particular position, any material reduction in rank constitutes a breach of the employment agreement and is tantamount to a discharge.

Miller v. Winshall, 400 N.E.2d 1306 (Mass.App. 1980)

16

Layoffs

Discipline is not the only reason why an employee might be terminated. An employee or group of employees might be let go purely for economic reasons, such as a cost-savings measure, elimination of a product line, job restructuring, reorganization, merger with a competitor, or similar reasons having nothing to do with employee performance or behavior. Again, the employer must be able to identify and articulate the business-related reason for the termination.

A reorganization or job elimination cannot be used as a pretext to get rid of an employee who might otherwise be in a protected status.

Example

A pregnant employee in the Compliance Department of a New York securities firm requested leave under the *Family and Medical Leave Act*. Until that time, she had received periodic raises, promotions, and compliments on her work. While she was on leave, the firm promoted a part-time employee in the Compliance Department to full-time, and assigned the newly promoted employee most of the duties that the pregnant employee had been performing. Two weeks before the employee on FMLA leave was to return, the firm fired her and sent her a severance

(continued)

package. When asked why she was being fired, the firm explained that it was part of a corporate downsizing and that she was among those chosen for termination because of her poor performance. She then sued the securities firm, claiming discrimination because of sex and retaliation for taking FMLA leave. A federal trial court ruled that the circumstances surrounding the employee's dismissal gave rise to an inference of discrimination and it allowed her suit to proceed.

Batka v. Prime Charter, Ltd., 301 F. Supp. 2d 308 (S.D.N.Y. 2004)

Reductions-in-Force and Mass Layoffs

Terminating a single employee carries some risk. Laying off a significant portion of the workforce increases the risk many times over. Particularly in tough economic times, laid-off employees will have more difficulty finding new employment, so their incentive to sue (along with spare time to discuss and plan a lawsuit) is even greater.

When considering a mass layoff, the following steps will help reduce the risk.

- ◆ Consider other *cost-saving alternatives* to a layoff, such as offering wage rate or hour reductions to employees.
- ◆ Develop and document the *business reasons* for the layoff.
- ◆ Focus on *positions*, not *people*, to be eliminated.
- ◆ Hire an *outside expert* to help decide what positions to eliminate.
- ◆ Make sure that layoff decisions are not influenced in any way by *discriminatory factors*, such as race, gender, or age.
- ◆ Once tentative layoff decisions have been made, and assuming the decisions have not been *intentionally* influenced by discriminatory factors, use an outside expert to review the *unintended* impact along race, gender, and age lines.

◆ Offer severance packages, early retirement packages, or other *exit incentives* in exchange for a release of all claims, but be sure to comply with the special requirements of the Age *Discrimination in Employment* Act (discussed in Chapter 4).

◆ Follow customary *exit interviews* and procedures for each individual being laid off.

The federal *Worker Adjustment and Retraining Notification Act* (WARN) requires an employer with 100 or more employees to provide notification 60 days in advance of a planned plant closing or mass layoff. In determining whether an employer meets the 100-employee floor, only full-time employees are counted. However, if part-timers work at least 4,000 hours per week in the aggregate, part-timers are counted as well.

A *mass layoff* for WARN purposes is a layoff of at least 50 employees at a single site, which amounts to at least 33% of the employees at that site. So if an employer has 1,000 employees at a given site and lays off 100, that would not be a mass layoff. Neither would a layoff of 40 employees out of a total workforce of 60.

The 60-day notice must be given to the affected employees, to the state dislocated worker unit, and to the chief elected official of the local government where the plant closing or layoff is to occur. Advance notice provides workers and their families some transition time to adjust to the prospective loss of employment, to seek and obtain alternative jobs, and if necessary, to enter skill training or retraining that will allow these workers to successfully compete in the job market.

The WARN Act recognizes that in some circumstances, it may not be possible for employers to give the requisite notice. The Act's so-called *unforeseeable business circumstances exception* is applicable when a similarly situated employer, exercising commercially reasonable business judgment, would not have foreseen the closing. In other words, an employer who is exercising reasonable business judgment will not be held liable under WARN for failing to predict economic or other conditions that may affect demand for its products or services.

Example

A Michigan automobile parts manufacturer had a contract to supply parts to another company. The contract was renegotiated every year. Shortly before one such agreement was due to expire, officials of the manufacturer and the customer met and the customer assured the manufacturer that the agreement would be renewed. In fact, the agreement did not get renewed, so the manufacturer continued production on a month-to-month basis.

While discussions between the two companies were ongoing, the customer was also negotiating with another supplier. The manufacturer was aware of these negotiations, but believed itself to be the only viable supplier and was assured that was so. When one of the customer's payments did not arrive as scheduled, an official of the manufacturer asked to pick up the check. The official was then informed for the first time that the customer was not going to pay and that it would cease doing business with the manufacturer. The manufacturer was immediately forced to close its doors without giving the requisite 60-day notice under WARN.

A federal appeals court ruled that the closing was the result of sudden and unexpected actions taken by the customer that the manufacturer could not reasonably have foreseen. Therefore, the closing fell within the exception to WARN's notice requirement.

Watson v. Michigan Industrial Holdings, Inc., 311 F.3d 760 (6th Cir. 2002)

17

Protected Status

The term *at-will employment* has been defined at various places in this book as a relationship that either party can terminate at any time for any reason or for no reason. But the definition has always included the caveat, *except for an illegal reason.*

Discrimination is one of those illegal reasons. As discussed in Chapter 4, an employer cannot take an adverse employment action based on an individual's race, color, religion, sex, age, disability, and a host of other criteria listed in federal, state, and local discrimination laws. Although Chapter 4 covered discrimination in *hiring*, it is just as illegal for an employer to *fire* for a discriminatory reason.

Another illegal reason is a discharge that violates the terms of a contract between the employer and the employee. (see Chapter 11.)

This chapter and the next few chapters address other illegal reasons that constitute additional exceptions to at-will employment. This chapter covers protected leave, Chapter 18 looks at retaliation, Chapter 19 discusses strikes and concerted activities, and Chapter 20 examines claims of wrongful discharge.

There are a number of circumstances in which an employee cannot be fired for being absent from work, even though the employee's inability to work would normally justify termination.

Family and Medical Leave

The *Family and Medical Leave Act* (FMLA) applies to employers who have 50 or more employees for at least twenty weeks during the current or preceding calendar year. (Chapter 3 tells how to count employees for statutory threshold purposes.) An employee is potentially eligible for FMLA leave if he or she:

- works for a covered employer;
- has been on the job for a year or more;
- has worked at least 1250 hours during the previous year; and,
- works at a location where there are at least fifty employees within seventy miles.

When leave qualifies under FMLA, a covered employer must:

- grant an eligible employee up to twelve weeks of unpaid leave, including intermittent leave as needed, within a twelve-month period;
- restore the employee to his or her former job or to an *equivalent job* (a job that is virtually identical to the former job in terms of pay, benefits, and other employment terms and conditions) upon return to work; and,
- maintain group health insurance coverage for the employee, including family coverage, on the same basis as if the employee had continued to work.

The only exception to the duty to grant FMLA leave is for *key employees* whose absence would cause *substantial and grievous economic injury to the operations of the employer.* This is defined as a salaried, eligible employee who is among the highest paid 10% of the employees employed by the employer within seventy-five miles of the facility at which the employee is employed. If the employer intends to deny leave on this basis, the employer must first notify the affected employee and give the employee an opportunity to change his or her mind about taking FMLA leave.

Example

Moira requested and received maternity leave from her employer. When she requested an extension of that leave, her employer informed her by letter that she was a key employee under FMLA and that her position could be filled permanently during her absence. Moira took the letter as a termination and sued for severance benefits to which she was entitled under her employment contract upon termination. A federal trial court in Pennsylvania found that Moira was in fact a key employee and that in her absence the employer was suffering substantial and grievous economic injury. (The company filed for bankruptcy shortly after this incident.) The court also found that the letter was not a termination, but was issued to comply with FMLA's notice requirement. Therefore, Moira was not terminated and was not entitled to severance.

Kelly v. DecisionOne Corp., 2000 WL 1843409 (E.D.Pa. 2000),

aff'd, 276 F.3d 577 (3d Cir. 2001)

An eligible employee is entitled to FMLA leave when the employee:

- has a serious health condition;
- needs to care for a spouse, child, or parent with a serious health condition;
- needs to care for a newborn child; or,
- adopts a child or has a child placed with the employee for foster care.

Serious health condition is defined as an illness, injury, impairment, or physical or mental condition that involves:

- treatment as an in-patient in a hospital, hospice, or residential medical care facility;

- a period of incapacity requiring absence of more than three days from work, school, or other regular activity *and* that involves continuing treatment by a health-care provider;

- any period of incapacity due to pregnancy or for prenatal care;

- any period of incapacity due to a chronic, serious health condition;

- a period of incapacity that is permanent or long-term, even if there is no effective treatment; or,

- absences to receive multiple treatment in which the underlying condition, if left untreated, would likely result in incapacity of more than three consecutive days.

U.S. Department of Labor regulations expand on the statutory definition. DOL regs say that a condition qualifies as serious if the employee is incapacitated for more than three consecutive calendar days and the condition requires treatment two or more times by a health-care practitioner. Even the flu can satisfy this test, according to a federal appeals court decision.

Example

Margaret worked in Patient Accounts at a hospital in Florida. She had a history of being disciplined for unscheduled absences. In May 2000, Margaret fell at work, breaking her elbow and ankle and spraining her wrist. She was referred to the hospital-approved workers' compensation health-care provider for treatment and did not return to work that day. Over the next few days she did report to work, but in each case left after

(continued)

---

a few hours, complaining of severe pain or of nausea from the painkillers she was taking. She also missed time for follow-up doctor's appointments. Eventually the hospital fired her.

Margaret sued, claiming the hospital had retaliated against her for taking FMLA leave. To prove retaliation, however, Margaret first had to show that she had a serious health condition and was entitled to FMLA leave. She based her proof on the fact that she was incapacitated for *portions of* more than three consecutive calendar days. The hospital disputed Margaret's claim, arguing that the regulatory language *three consecutive calendar days* means *three full* days (72 hours). A federal appeals court sided with the hospital, ruling that the period of incapacity must be continuous for more than three days and that partial days of incapacity do not count.

Russell v. North Broward Hosp., 346 F.3d 1335 (11th Cir. 2003)

When an employee requests FMLA leave, the employer must respond promptly. Optional Form WH-381 may be used for this purpose. (A sample can be found on the following page.)

An employer may require a medical certification of the serious health condition from a health-care provider, but must allow the employee fifteen days to obtain the certification. The employer may, at its own expense, obtain a second opinion from another health-care provider of the employer's own choosing, so long as the health-care provider is not under contract with, or regularly used by, the employer. If the two opinions differ, the employer and employee together choose a third health-care provider, whose opinion is final and binding. Optional Form WH-380 may be used for these medical certifications. (A sample can be found on pages 158–161.)

For more information on FMLA, go to **www.dol.gov/esa/whd/fmla/index.htm**.

Employer Response to Employee Request for Family or Medical Leave *(Optional Use Form -- See 29 CFR § 825.301)*	**U.S. Department of Labor** Employment Standards Administration Wage and Hour Division	

(Family and Medical Leave Act of 1993)

Date:

OMB No. : 1215-0181
Expires : 08-31-07

To: _____
(Employee's Name)

From: _____
(Name of Appropriate Employer Representative)

Subject: REQUEST FOR FAMILY/MEDICAL LEAVE

On _____ , you notified us of your need to take family/medical leave due to:
(Date)

☐   The birth of a child, or the placement of a child with you for adoption or foster care; or

☐   A serious health condition that makes you unable to perform the essential functions for your job: or

☐   A serious health condition affecting your ☐ spouse, ☐ child, ☐ parent, for which you are needed to provide care.

You notified us that you need this leave beginning on _____ and that you expect
(Date)

leave to continue until on or about _____ .
(Date)

Except as explained below, you have a right under the FMLA for up to 12 weeks of unpaid leave in a 12-month period for the reasons listed above. Also, your health benefits must be maintained during any period of unpaid leave under the same conditions as if you continued to work, and you must be reinstated to the same or an equivalent job with the same pay, benefits, and terms and conditions of employment on your return from leave. If you do not return to work following FMLA leave for a reason other than: (1) the continuation, recurrence, or onset of a serious health condition which would entitle you to FMLA leave; or (2) other circumstances beyond your control, you may be required to reimburse us for our share of health insurance premiums paid on your behalf during your FMLA leave.

This is to inform you that: *(check appropriate boxes; explain where indicated)*

1. You are ☐ eligible ☐ not eligible for leave under the FMLA.

2. The requested leave ☐ will ☐ will not be counted against your annual FMLA leave entitlement.

3. You ☐ will ☐ will not be required to furnish medical certification of a serious health condition. If required, you must furnish certification by _____ *(insert date)* (must be at least 15 days after you are notified of this requirement), or we may delay the commencement of your leave until the certification is submitted.

4. You may elect to substitute accrued paid leave for unpaid FMLA leave. We ☐ will ☐ will not require that you substitute accrued paid leave for unpaid FMLA leave. If paid leave will be used, the following conditions will apply: *(Explain)*

Form WH-381
Rev. June 1997

Employer Response to Employee
Request for Family or Medical Leave
(Optional Use Form -- See 29 CFR § 825.301)

U.S. Department of Labor
Employment Standards Administration
Wage and Hour Division

(Family and Medical Leave Act of 1993)

OMB No. : 1215-0181
Expires : 08-31-07

Date:

To: _____
(Employee's Name)

From: _____
(Name of Appropriate Employer Representative)

Subject: REQUEST FOR FAMILY/MEDICAL LEAVE

On _____ , you notified us of your need to take family/medical leave due to:
(Date)

☐ The birth of a child, or the placement of a child with you for adoption or foster care; or

☐ A serious health condition that makes you unable to perform the essential functions for your job: or

☐ A serious health condition affecting your ☐ spouse, ☐ child, ☐ parent, for which you are needed to provide care.

You notified us that you need this leave beginning on _____ and that you expect
(Date)

leave to continue until on or about _____ .
(Date)

Except as explained below, you have a right under the FMLA for up to 12 weeks of unpaid leave in a 12-month period for the reasons listed above. Also, your health benefits must be maintained during any period of unpaid leave under the same conditions as if you continued to work, and you must be reinstated to the same or an equivalent job with the same pay, benefits, and terms and conditions of employment on your return from leave. If you do not return to work following FMLA leave for a reason other than: (1) the continuation, recurrence, or onset of a serious health condition which would entitle you to FMLA leave; or (2) other circumstances beyond your control, you may be required to reimburse us for our share of health insurance premiums paid on your behalf during your FMLA leave.

This is to inform you that: *(check appropriate boxes; explain where indicated)*

1. You are ☐ eligible ☐ not eligible for leave under the FMLA.

2. The requested leave ☐ will ☐ will not be counted against your annual FMLA leave entitlement.

3. You ☐ will ☐ will not be required to furnish medical certification of a serious health condition. If required, you must furnish certification by _____ *(insert date)* (must be at least 15 days after you are notified of this requirement), or we may delay the commencement of your leave until the certification is submitted.

4. You may elect to substitute accrued paid leave for unpaid FMLA leave. We ☐ will ☐ will not require that you substitute accrued paid leave for unpaid FMLA leave. If paid leave will be used, the following conditions will apply: *(Explain)*

Form WH-381

157

Certification of Health Care Provider (Family and Medical Leave Act of 1993)	**U.S. Department of Labor** Employment Standards Administration Wage and Hour Division

*(When completed, this form goes to the employee, **Not to the Department of Labor**.)*		OMB No.: 1215-0181 Expires: 07/31/07

1. Employee's Name

2. Patient's Name *(If different from employee)*

3. Page 4 describes what is meant by a **"serious health condition"** under the Family and Medical Leave Act. Does the patient's condition[1] qualify under any of the categories described? If so, please check the applicable category.

(1) _____ (2) _____ (3) _____ (4) _____ (5) _____ (6) _____ , or None of the above _____

4. Describe the **medical facts** which support your certification, including a brief statement as to how the medical facts meet the criteria of one of these categories:

5. a. State the approximate **date** the condition commenced, and the probable duration of the condition (and also the probable duration of the patient's present **incapacity**[2] if different):

b. Will it be necessary for the employee to take work only **intermittently or to work on a less than full schedule** as a result of the condition (including for treatment described in Item 6 below)?

If yes, give the probable duration:

c. If the condition is a **chronic condition** (condition #4) or **pregnancy**, state whether the patient is presently incapacitated[2] and the likely duration and frequency of **episodes of incapacity**[2]:

[1] Here and elsewhere on this form, the information sought relates **only** to the condition for which the employee is taking FMLA leave.

[2] "Incapacity," for purposes of FMLA, is defined to mean inability to work, attend school or perform other regular daily activities due to the serious health condition, treatment therefor, or recovery therefrom.

Form WH-380
Revised December 1999

If the patient will be absent from work or other daily activities because of **treatment** on an **intermittent** or **part-time** basis, also provide an estimate of the probable number of and interval between such treatments, actual or estimated dates of treatment if known, and period required for recovery if any:

b. If any of these treatments will be provided by **another provider of health services** (e.g., physical therapist), please state the nature of the treatments:

c. **If a regimen of continuing treatment** by the patient is required under your supervision, provide a general description of such regimen (*e.g.*, prescription drugs, physical therapy requiring special equipment):

7. a. If medical leave is required for the employee's **absence from work** because of the **employee's own condition** (including absences due to pregnancy or a chronic condition), is the employee **unable to perform work** of any kind?

b. If able to perform some work, is the employee **unable to perform any one or more of the essential functions of the employee's job** (the employee or the employer should supply you with information about the essential job functions)? If yes, please list the essential functions the employee is unable to perform:

c. If neither a. nor b. applies, is it necessary for the employee to be **absent from work for treatment**?

8. a. If leave is required to **care for a family member** of the employee with a serious health condition, **does the patient require assistance** for basic medical or personal needs or safety, or for transportation?

   b. If no, would the employee's presence to provide **psychological comfort** be beneficial to the patient or assist in the patient's recovery?

   c. If the patient will need care only **intermittently** or on a part-time basis, please indicate the probable **duration** of this need:

Signature of Health Care Provider   Type of Practice

Address   Telephone Number

                                                                         Date

To be completed by the employee needing family leave to care for a family member:

State the care you will provide and an estimate of the period during which care will be provided, including a schedule if leave is to be taken intermittently or if it will be necessary for you to work less than a full schedule:

Employee Signature   Date

A **"Serious Health Condition"** means an illness, injury impairment, or physical or mental condition that involves one of the following:

1. Hospital Care

   Inpatient care (*i.e.*, an overnight stay) in a hospital, hospice, or residential medical care facility, including any period of incapacity[2] or subsequent treatment in connection with or consequent to such inpatient care.

2. Absence Plus Treatment

   (a) A period of incapacity[2] of **more than three consecutive calendar days** (including any subsequent treatment or period of incapacity[2] relating to the same condition), that also involves:

   (1) **Treatment**[3] **two or more times** by a health care provider, by a nurse or physician's assistant under direct supervision of a health care provider, or by a provider of health care services (*e.g.*, physical therapist) under orders of, or on referral by, a health care provider; or

   (2) **Treatment** by a health care provider on **at least one occasion** which results in a **regimen of continuing treatment**[4] under the supervision of the health care provider.

3. Pregnancy

   Any period of incapacity due to **pregnancy**, or for **prenatal care**.

4. Chronic Conditions Requiring Treatments

   A **chronic condition** which:

   (1) Requires **periodic visits** for treatment by a health care provider, or by a nurse or physician's assistant under direct supervision of a health care provider;

   (2) Continues over an **extended period of time** (including recurring episodes of a single underlying condition); and

   (3) May cause **episodic** rather than a continuing period of incapacity[2] (*e.g.*, asthma, diabetes, epilepsy, etc.).

5. Permanent/Long-term Conditions Requiring Supervision

   A period of **Incapacity**[2] which is **permanent or long-term** due to a condition for which treatment may not be effective. The employee or family member must be **under the continuing supervision of, but need not be receiving active treatment by, a health care provider**. Examples include Alzheimer's, a severe stroke, or the terminal stages of a disease.

6. Multiple Treatments (Non-Chronic Conditions)

   Any period of absence to receive **multiple treatments** (including any period of recovery therefrom) by a health care provider or by a provider of health care services under orders of, or on referral by, a health care provider, either for **restorative surgery** after an accident or other injury, **or** for a condition that **would likely result in a period of Incapacity**[2] **of more than three consecutive calendar days in the absence of medical intervention or treatment**, such as cancer (chemotherapy, radiation, etc.), severe arthritis (physical therapy), and kidney disease (dialysis).

This optional form may be used by employees to satisfy a mandatory requirement to furnish a medical certification (when requested) from a health care provider, including second or third opinions and recertification (29 CFR 825.306).

Note: Persons are not required to respond to this collection of information unless it displays a currently valid OMB control number.

---

[3] Treatment includes examinations to determine if a serious health condition exists and evaluations of the condition. Treatment does not include routine physical examinations, eye examinations, or dental examinations.

[4] A regimen of continuing treatment includes, for example, a course of prescription medication (*e.g.*, an antibiotic) or therapy requiring special equipment to resolve or alleviate the health condition. A regimen of treatment does not include the taking of over-the-counter medications such as aspirin, antihistamines, or salves; or bed-rest, drinking fluids, exercise, and other similar activities that can be initiated without a visit to a health care provider.

Public Burden Statement

We estimate that it will take an average of 20 minutes to complete this collection of information, including the time for reviewing instructions, searching existing data sources, gathering and maintaining the data needed, and completing and reviewing the collection of information. If you have any comments regarding this burden estimate or any other aspect of this collection of information, including suggestions for reducing this burden, send them to the Administrator, Wage and Hour Division, Department of Labor, Room S-3502, 200 Constitution Avenue, N.W., Washington, D.C. 20210.

DO NOT SEND THE COMPLETED FORM TO THIS OFFICE; IT GOES TO THE EMPLOYEE.

---

*U.S. GPO: 2000-461-954/25505

Firing an Employee on FMLA Leave

While an employee cannot be fired *because* he or she requested FMLA leave, or *in retaliation for* taking FMLA leave, an employee may be fired *while on* FMLA leave if the employee would have been fired regardless of his or her FMLA leave status.

Example

An employee at a Tennessee automobile manufacturer approached his supervisor and explained that his wife was expecting, that she would be delivering within the month, and that he needed some time off. When the baby did arrive, the employee called his supervisor and asked for four weeks' leave, which the supervisor approved. It turned out that one of the reasons the employee wanted leave was to fill in as manager of his wife's restaurant while she tended to their newborn child, even though the manufacturer had a strict policy against their workers performing any outside work while on leave. When the manufacturer discovered this, it fired him for violating company policy. A federal appeals court upheld the termination, pointing out that the right to reinstatement is not absolute, since an employer need not reinstate an employee who would have lost his or her job even without taking FMLA leave. Because the employee here was fired for violating a company policy unrelated to FMLA, he could not claim protection under the statute.

Pharakhone v. Nissan North America, Inc., 324 F.3d 405 (6th Cir. 2003)

Misconduct that occurs *before* FMLA leave can also justify discipline *while* an employee is out on leave. In other words, FMLA does not require an employer to suspend its normal policies just because an employee has qualified for leave. A county police department in Maryland, for example, was not prevented from going forward with a disciplinary hearing against one of its officers accused of earlier misconduct, even though the hearing occurred while he was on FMLA leave.

Military Leave

The *Uniformed Services Employment and Reemployment Rights Act* (USERRA), adopted in 1994, requires employers to carry service members on leave status for benefit and seniority purposes while on active duty and to reemploy them when they return. USERRA also prohibits employers from discriminating against veterans and persons in the uniformed services. USERRA applies to all service members, except those who receive dishonorable or bad conduct discharges or who are discharged under less than honorable conditions.

To be eligible for USERRA protection, the service member must notify his or her employer that he or she has been called to active duty, unless precluded from doing so by military necessity or unless it is otherwise impossible or unreasonable to do so. Employees on active duty are considered to be on furlough or leave of absence. As such, they are entitled to whatever benefits other similarly situated employees receive. In addition, an employee on active duty:

- ◆ may (but cannot be required to) use any accrued vacation or other leave with pay;
- ◆ may elect to continue any employer-sponsored health insurance coverage for up to eighteen months (for employees on active duty for less than thirty-one days, the employee can only be required to pay the portion of the premium normally charged to employees; for employees on active duty for more than thirty days, the employee can be charged up to 102% of the full premium);
- ◆ may continue to contribute to any retirement plan to which he or she was contributing prior to active duty; and,

♦ must be treated as continuing to work for his or her employer for purposes of computing the employer's pension plan funding obligation and benefits under any pension plan in which he or she participates.

A returning service member is entitled to be reemployed unless the employer can show that the employer's circumstances have so changed as to make reemployment impossible or unreasonable, or that reemployment would impose an undue hardship. This right applies to service members who have been on active duty for as long a five years, and in some cases, even longer.

The returning service member is entitled to be placed in the position in which he or she would have been employed but for the call to active duty (or in a position with equivalent seniority, status, and pay). Under this *escalator* provision, the employer must take into consideration any promotions or advancements the member would have received if he or she had continued to work. If a member who has been on active duty for more than ninety days is not qualified for an escalated position, the employer must make reasonable efforts to help the member become qualified. For returning service members who became disabled while on active duty, the employer must make reasonable efforts to accommodate the disability.

To be eligible for reemployment, the returning service member must, after release from active duty, notify the employer of his or her intent to return to work. Strict time limits apply to this notice requirement.

♦ If the period of active duty was less than 31 days, the returning member must report to work on the first regular workday after his or her release from duty (after allowing for an eight-hour rest period and safe transportation home).

♦ If the period of active duty was between 31 and 181 days, the returning member must apply for reemployment within fourteen days after release from duty.

◆ If the period of active duty was more than 180 days, the returning member must apply for reemployment within ninety days after release from duty.

These time limits can be extended for up to two years or more in cases of returning service members who are hospitalized or convalescing from an illness or injury suffered while on active duty.

Once the employer has reemployed a returning service member, it is restricted in its ability to discharge the member. Except for discharges for cause, members who have been on active duty for 180 days or less cannot be fired for a period of 180 days after reemployment. Members who have been on active duty for more than 180 days cannot be fired for one year.

(For more information on USERRA, go to **www.dol.gov/dol/compliance/ comp-userra.htm**.)

Jury Duty

Federal law prohibits employers from discharging, threatening to discharge, intimidating, or coercing any permanent employee by reason of the employee's jury service in federal court. Almost all states have similar provisions protecting employees who are serving as jurors in state court. (Montana appears to be the only exception at this writing.) Some states even require employers to continue paying their employees while on jury duty, or at least pay the difference between the employee's regular pay and the fees he or she receives for jury service. (A summary of state laws regarding jury service is available at **www.toolkit.cch.com/text/P05_4340.asp**.)

Some—but not all—states also protect the jobs of persons who are subpoenaed as witnesses in court proceedings or who attend criminal court proceedings under a victims' rights law.

Unless state law requires otherwise, it is permissible for an employer not to pay an employee who is on jury duty or attending court as a witness. However, if the employee is *exempt* from overtime requirements under the *Fair Labor Standards Act*, failure to pay at least the difference between the regular salary and the juror or witness fees the employee receives may result in that employee's being reclassified as *nonexempt*.

18

Retaliation

Virtually all federal worker protection laws contain nonretaliation provisions. For example:

◆ *Title VII* of the federal *Civil Rights Act* does not only prohibit discrimination in employment because of an individual's race, color, religion, sex, or national origin. It also prohibits retaliation against an employee who has complained about discrimination or who has assisted another complainant, such as by testifying on his or her behalf.

◆ The *Fair Labor Standards Act* (FLSA), which requires employers to pay minimum wages and time-and-a-half for overtime to their nonexempt employees, contains nonretaliation provisions similar to Title VII.

◆ The *Family and Medical Leave Act* (FMLA) prohibits interference with an employee's rights under the Act or disciplining him or her for filing a complaint or testifying.

◆ The *National Labor Relations Act* (NLRA) prohibits an employer from interfering with, restraining, or coercing employees in the exercise of their rights under the Act or from discharging or otherwise discriminating against an employee because he or she has filed charges or given testimony under the Act.

- The *Occupational Safety and Health Act* (OSHA) prohibits retaliation against an employee because the employee filed an OSHA complaint, testified in a OSHA proceeding, or exercised any other rights afforded by the statute.
- The *Employee Retirement Income Security Act* (ERISA), which regulates employee benefit plans, makes it unlawful to discharge, discipline, or discriminate against a plan participant or beneficiary for exercising any right to which he or she is entitled under a plan or for giving information or testifying in connection with an ERISA inquiry.

Comparable provisions are found in state and local worker protection laws.

Whenever an employee has exercised rights guaranteed by law, such as by filing a discrimination charge, employers should exercise extraordinary caution in making personnel decisions that would adversely affect the complaining employee or others involved in the matter. Any such action taken after the initial charge has been made is likely to generate a charge of retaliation.

Example

An engineer had worked at a hospital in Pennsylvania for seventeen years when he left his job. Claiming that he had been forced out of his job due to age and disability discrimination, he sued. The engineer's son also worked for the hospital as a security guard. According to the son, a hospital manager repeatedly questioned him about the status of his father's lawsuit in an attempt to pry information out of him to aid the hospital's defense. The son claimed that he had no involvement in the lawsuit and refused to answer any of the manager's questions. After eighteen years at the hospital, the son, too, was fired.

(continued)

According to the hospital, the firing was justified because the son had used a passkey without authorization to enter the hospital's gift shop. The son argued that the firing was a mere pretext, since he was authorized to use the passkey and had routinely done so in the past. The real reason, according to the son, was that the hospital thought he was helping with his father's lawsuit. In the son's suit, a federal appellate court ruled that the son stated a good claim for illegal retaliation. As the court pointed out, *to retaliate against a man by hurting a member of his family is an ancient method of revenge, and is not unknown in the field of labor relations.*

Fogleman v. Mercy Hosp., Inc., 283 F.3d 561 (3rd Cir. 2002)

Retaliation claims often become the tail wagging the dog. An employee may have a weak or improbable claim of race or sex discrimination. But when he or she complains and the employer responds by firing the employee, the employer has effectively converted a weak claim that the employee would probably have lost into a strong claim of retaliation that the employee will likely win. An employee cannot, however, intentionally file false charges and expect protection from retaliation, as the following example shows.

Example

An electrician at a manufacturing facility in Illinois was apparently not comfortable working for a female supervisor. The supervisor also reported him once for sleeping on the job and again for leaving some equipment unattended. Several days after the second incident, the electrician complained that one of the supervisor's breasts had touched him while the two of them were having a conversation in a work area. He also complained that the supervisor had reached around him to retrieve a tool, although no actual touching occurred that time.

(continued)

When the company's Equal Employment Opportunity Officer investigated his complaints, the electrician told the EEO Officer that he did not know whether the supervisor had touched him in a suggestive way. He also said that the contact might have been inadvertent and he did not believe the supervisor was attracted to him. Based on these statements, the investigator concluded that the complaint was without merit.

Three months later, the electrician filed charges of sexual harassment with the Equal Employment Opportunity Commission and the Illinois Department of Human Rights. Those charges triggered a further investigation by the company, during which another employee stated under oath that the touching incident never occurred and that the electrician's goal was to get rid of his supervisor. With this additional information in hand, the company fired the electrician for dishonesty. The electrician sued, claiming retaliation. A federal appeals court ruled that the electrician's complaint was completely groundless, frivolous, and motivated by bad faith. In those circumstances, said the court, the electrician lost any protection from retaliation and was justifiably fired.

Mattson v. Caterpillar, Inc., 359 F.3d 885 (7th Cir. 2004)

Employee Benefits

As noted, the *Employee Retirement Income Security Act* (ERISA) makes it unlawful to discharge, discipline, or discriminate against a plan participant or beneficiary for exercising any right to which he or she is entitled under a plan or for giving information or testifying in connection with an ERISA inquiry. It is also unlawful under ERISA for an employer to *interfere with the attainment of any right* to which a participant may become entitled under the plan. This means that an employer cannot fire an employee in order to prevent him or her from becoming vested in a retirement plan or in order to reduce the amount of benefits that might otherwise be available.

> **Example**
>
> A Wisconsin farm equipment manufacturer fired one of its employees after he had worked there almost thirty years and shortly before he was to become eligible for early retirement. The discharge did not affect his basic pension, which was fully vested, but it did prevent him from becoming eligible for additional benefits. Believing that the company acted for the purpose of interfering with attainment of those additional benefits, the employee sued under ERISA. The trial court dismissed the suit, reasoning that the benefits at issue were not then vested and that since the employer retained the power to amend the plan and eliminate those benefits, it necessarily had the power to fire the employee to prevent him from attaining the benefits. A federal appeals court reversed and sent the case back for trial. The appellate court ruled that ERISA protects unvested as well as vested benefits, and that the power to amend a plan does not allow an employer to interfere with a particular employee's benefits, whether vested or not.
>
> *Heath v. Varity Corp., 71 F.3d 256 (7th Cir. 1995)*

Whistleblowing

Persons who go public with violations of law by their employers, particularly violations involving fraud against the government, are known as *whistleblowers*. In the absence of specific statutory protections, whistleblowers may find themselves out of a job, with little right to complain. However, a number of jurisdictions have decided that whistleblowers should receive some limited protection.

A pre-Civil War federal statute known as the *False Claims Act* permits anyone who learns about fraud against the U.S. government to file a lawsuit in the name of the government. The Act provides an incentive to sue by allowing persons who bring the suit to collect a percentage of any recovery.

When the person bringing the suit is an employee of the company accused of fraud, a provision of the Act prohibits the company from firing the employee or otherwise retaliating against him or her.

Additional statutory protection is contained in a Reconstruction-era civil rights law that prohibits persons from conspiring to force, intimidate, or threaten witnesses in federal court proceedings. In a case involving a grand jury investigation of a company accused of Medicare fraud, the Supreme Court held that an employee of the company, who was fired for cooperating with the grand jury, could sue for damages under the statute even though he was an at-will employee.

Some states have enacted their own whistleblower laws protecting employees who disclose government fraud at the state level.

Financial Difficulties

The federal *Bankruptcy Act* prohibits employers from terminating or otherwise discriminating against an individual who has filed for bankruptcy or who has failed to pay a debt that has been discharged in bankruptcy. Federal law and the laws of some states also prohibit firing an employee for a first-time garnishment of wages.

Sarbanes-Oxley

The rash of recent corporate scandals by publicly traded companies has prompted Congress to pass tough new legislation. Although the *Sarbanes-Oxley Act of 2002* focuses primarily on accounting oversight and corporate governance, the Act contains a number of provisions that directly affect high-level—and in some cases, lower-echelon—employees of publicly-traded companies. Under the Act, it is now criminal for a company to retaliate against an employee who assists in any investigation by federal regulators, Congress, or company supervisors, or who provides information to federal law enforcement officers. Any person who suffers unlawful retaliation may also initiate a civil suit for reinstatement, backpay, and other damages.

Work-Related Injuries and Illnesses

Workers' compensation acts are no-fault laws under which the employer is automatically obligated to pay compensation and benefits for any employee who suffers a work-related illness or injury. The trade-off for the employer is that workers' compensation benefits are the employee's *exclusive remedy*.

Since workers' compensation benefits are the employee's only remedy, it makes sense that an injured employee who takes advantage of that remedy and files a claim for benefits will be protected from retaliation by his or her employer. And that is exactly what the courts have ruled—an employer cannot fire an employee or take other adverse action against him or her *because he or she has filed a workers' compensation claim.*

But what if the employee is fired not because he or she filed a claim, but because he or she is simply not at work? Suppose an employer has an across-the-board policy that any employee who is incapacitated for more than two weeks is subject to being terminated and having his or her position filled by a permanent replacement. Suppose also that the employer can show a legitimate business reason for such a policy and can show that the policy is applied evenhandedly, regardless of whether the incapacity is work-related. Should the employer not be allowed to enforce its policy, even as to employees who are out on temporary total disability and receiving workers' comp benefits?

For the most part, the courts have agreed with the employer on this issue. They have ruled that an employer has no duty to carry an employee who does not show up for work, even if the reason he or she does not show up is a work-related disability.

A small minority of states—most notably, Ohio and Kansas—go the other way. In a recent decision, the Ohio Supreme Court said that a rule prohibiting such terminations is necessary to protect the rights of employees to freely pursue workers' compensation benefits without fear of reprisal. Under this minority view, getting terminated for being out of work is really no different from getting terminated for filing a workers' compensation claim—either way, the employer is illegally discouraging its employee from pursuing a statutory right to benefits.

Virginia, by statute, limits an employer's right to fire for excessive absenteeism when the absence is due to a compensable injury or illness.

Even where dismissal is otherwise permitted, firing an employee who is out on work-related disability is fraught with peril.

- ◆ The employee may argue that the termination was abusive or in retaliation for his or her having filed a workers' compensation claim. In order to defeat such an argument, the employer would have to show that it has an across-the-board policy of discharging *all* disabled employees and that it applies the policy evenhandedly for both work-related and non-work-related disabilities.
- ◆ The employee may be entitled to leave under the federal Family and Medical Leave Act or under a state law counterpart of FMLA.
- ◆ If the disabling condition is not merely temporary and if it substantially limits one or more major life activities, the employer's duty of reasonable accommodation under the Americans with Disabilities Act or state law may be triggered.

Former Employees

Even though independent contractors are not covered by employment discrimination laws, the granting or withholding of such work to former employees, when motivated by discrimination, is illegal.

Example

Thomas had worked for a trade association in Illinois for twenty-two years before he was fired. At the time of his termination, the association offered him a severance package consisting of cash, continuing health benefits, and a consulting arrangement. Believing he was terminated because of his age (63) and because he was disabled by heart disease, complicated by sleep apnea, Thomas filed discrimination charges with the EEOC. When the association learned of those charges, it withdrew the offer to enter into a consulting arrangement. Thomas then filed an additional charge of retaliation.

In analyzing the retaliation claim, a federal appeals court began with the proposition that the *Age Discrimination in Employment Act* and the ADA do not protect independent contractors, which is what Thomas's status would have been as a consultant to the association. However, said the court, Thomas was not suing as an independent contractor, but as a former employee—and former employees, insofar as they are complaining of retaliation that impinges on their future employment prospects, do have a right to sue their former employers.

Flannery v. Recording Ind. Ass'n of America, 354 F.3d 632 (7th Cir. 2004)

19

Strikes and Concerted Activities

The *National Labor Relations Act* (NLRA) gives employees the right of self-organization, to form, join, or assist labor organizations, to bargain collectively through representatives of their own choosing, and to engage in other *concerted activities* for the purpose of collective bargaining or other mutual aid or protection. This includes the *right to strike*, which the courts have characterized as a legitimate economic tool that labor unions may use as they see fit. Any interference with those rights, such as by firing employees for engaging in union activities, is an unfair labor practice.

The right to engage in concerted activities also protects employees who are not unionized, and it protects activities that have nothing to do with the formation of a union. Examples of protected concerted activity, whether in a union or nonunion context, include the following.

- ◆ *Discussing wages and working conditions.* Since the right of employees to organize and bargain collectively necessarily encompasses the right to communicate with one another, an employer cannot adopt a rule prohibiting employees from discussing wages or other working conditions among themselves.

- ◆ *Discussing employee sexual harassment complaints.* The National Labor Relations Board has ruled that a company confidentiality requirement prohibiting discussion of a pending sexual harassment investigation is an unfair labor practice.

◆ *Inquiring about benefits.* Employees can be persistent in pursuing benefit claims so long as their conduct is not so flagrant or egregious as to interfere with company business practices.

◆ *Complaining about working conditions.* An employee cannot be disciplined for complaining to management about matters of common concern to all employees. Although the employee may initially be acting alone, his or her actions will be considered concerted so long as they are intended to initiate or induce group action. The intent to initiate or induce group action will be assumed if, for example, the complaint is voiced at a group meeting called to discuss working conditions.

◆ *Wearing pro-union buttons and insignia.* Wearing buttons and insignia is protected activity unless there are special considerations relating to employee efficiency and plant discipline.

◆ *Having a witness at a disciplinary hearing.* When an employer seeks to interview an employee in connection with a matter that could reasonably lead to discipline of the employee, and the employee requests the presence of a co-worker, the employer must either grant the employee's request and allow a co-worker to be present or cancel the interview.

Example

A trucking company entered into contracts with its long-haul truck drivers that required them to lease their trucks from the company and to make both substantial down payments and monthly lease payments. Although the contracts specified that the drivers were independent contractors, the contracts also gave the company the right to terminate the contractual arrangement at any time should a driver fail to meet company-imposed delivery schedules. In the event of termination, the drivers would forfeit

(continued)

their truck leases. The company also instructed the drivers to falsify their trip logs when necessary to make it appear that they had complied with federal regulations.

When two of the drivers became involved in union activities, the company terminated their contracts. Since the *National Labor Relations Act* does not protect independent contractors, the company claimed that its actions did not violate federal labor law. The National Labor Relations Board and a federal appeals court disagreed, ruling that while there were factors tending to support the company's position, the evidence on balance showed that the company's degree of control over the drivers made the drivers employees, not independent contractors. Therefore, the contract terminations constituted an unfair labor practice.

Time Auto Transportation, Inc. v. N.L.R.B., 377 F.3d 496 (6th Cir. 2004)

Replacing Striking Employees

When employees are engaged in an economic strike—a strike to improve wages, benefits, or other working conditions—the employer may hire permanent replacements, effectively firing the striking workers. However, when employees are engaged in a strike to protest unfair labor practices, the employer must reemploy them upon their making an unconditional offer to return to work.

Example

A family-owned newspaper in Pennsylvania used nonunion stringers (independent contractors) to handle certain overflow photography work without bargaining over the issue with its union. In response, the union voted to strike. During the striking workers' absence, the paper hired temporary replacements, but after negotiations between the paper and the union had continued off and on for a number of months, the paper

(continued)

179

> informed the union that the replacements were considered permanent. Sometime later, the striking workers made an unconditional offer to return to work, but the paper refused to take them back. A federal court of appeals ruled that, in assigning overflow work to nonunion stringers without first bargaining with the union over the assignment, the paper committed an unfair labor practice. The strike was, therefore, an unfair labor practice strike and the union workers were entitled to be reinstated.
>
> *Citizens Publishing & Printing Co. v. N.L.R.B., 263 F.3d 224 (3rd Cir. 2001)*

Partial Strikes

Rather than risk their jobs by striking to protest working conditions, employees sometimes engage in *job actions*, such as a slowdown, refusing to perform certain functions, or refusing to work overtime. Such job actions are not protected and they expose participating employees to termination.

Example

A Kentucky health-care provider operates nursing facilities and nursing homes at which it employs physical therapists, speech therapists, rehabilitation technicians, and aides. When the company announced that it would be reducing the wages of its rehabilitation employees, the affected employees established an informal group to protest the action. The group wrote a letter to management containing various demands, and it selected one of its members to represent them in a meeting with management. The group representative told the company's on-site supervisor that until someone from upper management met with the group to discuss their concerns, they would refuse to see patients and would only do paperwork. The supervisor responded by instructing all employees to continue seeing patients until the supervisor received guidance from upper management. When the employees refused to see patients as instructed, they were fired for insubordination.

(continued)

> The employees then filed unfair labor practice charges, but a federal appeals court upheld the firing. The court said that employees assume the risk of losing their jobs when they engage in an economic strike, but what they cannot do is strike and at the same time retain the benefits of working. Partial strikes, said the court, are not protected by federal labor law. The court explained that an employer has a right to know whether or not its employees are striking. Employees cannot refuse to perform certain work, either openly or secretly, while at the same time remaining on the employer's premises and demanding a paycheck.
>
> *Vencare Ancillary Services, Inc. v. N.L.R.B.,* 352 F.3d 318 (6th Cir. 2003)

Safety-Related Work Stoppages

Although the *Occupational Safety and Health Act* (OSHA) prohibits retaliation against an employee because the employee filed an OSHA complaint, the statute itself does not protect an employee who walks off the job out of safety concerns. In that situation, the employee's usual remedy is to notify his or her employer of the danger, and if the employer fails to take appropriate action, to request an OSHA inspection. The statute does not authorize unilateral self-help.

However, there may be situations in which the employee faces an impossible choice of either immediately complying with a supervisor's instructions and risking serious injury or death, or not complying and being fired. In those situations, the right to complain may simply not be a viable remedy. The U.S. Department of Labor has adopted regulations saying that if the employee—with no reasonable alternative—refuses (in good faith) to expose him- or herself to the dangerous condition, the employee will be protected from subsequent discipline.

The condition causing the employee's apprehension of death or injury must be of such a nature that a reasonable person would conclude that there is a real danger of death or serious injury and that there is insufficient time, due to the urgency of the situation, to eliminate the danger through resort to regular statutory enforcement channels. In addition, in such circumstances, the employee must also have sought from his or her employer, and been unable to obtain, a correction of the dangerous condition when possible.

In a 1980 decision, the Supreme Court upheld the Department of Labor's regulation in a case involving an employee who refused to work on a steel mesh that other workers had fallen through and suffered injury or death. Later court decisions have emphasized that the specific requirements of the regulation must be met—that the employee must be acting reasonably and in good faith, that the danger must be both real and serious, and that the employee must have had no opportunity to address the danger through regular channels.

The *National Labor Relations Act* (NLRA) also protects workers who voice safety concerns or who engage in a job action to protest safety conditions. Under the NLRA, an employer may not take adverse action against employees who engage in concerted activity by complaining about safety issues or other job-related conditions. The NLRA also provides that employees who quit work in the *good faith belief* that their workplace is *abnormally dangerous* are not deemed to be on strike. That provision has been interpreted to mean that, like workers who are on strike to protest an unfair labor practice, workers who are absent for safety reasons may not be permanently replaced.

In a 1962 Supreme Court decision involving a factory in Baltimore, seven employees walked off the job on a bitterly cold January day because their work area was unheated. The area was often uncomfortably cold anyway (a matter of repeated complaint) and, on the day in question, the furnace that usually supplied some heat had broken down. The Supreme Court ruled that the job action was protected under federal labor law, so that the employer had no right to fire the workers.

In more recent cases, fear of exposure to asbestos in an apartment complex and fear of exposure to radioactive depleted uranium dust have justified employee refusals to work.

20

Wrongful Discharge

The concept of *wrongful discharge* would seem to be completely incompatible with the employment-at-will doctrine. If an employer may fire an at-will employee at any time for any reason or for no reason, with or without cause, then how could a discharge ever be *wrongful?* The answer is that since the employment-at-will doctrine has been developed by court decisions as part of our common law, the courts feel free to fashion exceptions to the doctrine when doing so seems to serve the public interest.

Wrongful discharge (sometimes called *abusive discharge*) is closely related to *retaliation* and *whistleblowing*, discussed in previous chapters. In a retaliation or whistleblowing case, the *legislature*, by statute, grants certain rights to employees and prohibits employers from taking adverse action against the employee for exercising those rights. In a wrongful discharge case, there is no express statutory provision against retaliation. Instead, the *courts* conclude that allowing an employer to fire an employee would thwart a clear and important public policy, and that preservation of the public policy overrides an employer's right to fire.

Example

A truck driver in the District of Columbia was instructed by his employer to use a certain truck to make deliveries. The truck did not have an inspection

(continued)

sticker affixed to the windshield, as required by D.C. law, and driving the truck without the sticker would have been illegal. When the driver refused to drive the truck, he was fired. The driver then sued for wrongful discharge, claiming that to uphold his firing in these circumstances would undercut D.C. public policy as expressed in its motor vehicle laws. The D.C. Court of Appeals upheld the driver's claim and allowed him to recover both back wages and damages for emotional distress.

Adams v. George W. Cochran & Co., 597 A.2d 28 (D.C. 1991)

The wrongful discharge concept is sometimes described as a *narrow public policy exception* to the employment at will doctrine. But as the following example shows, the exception may be in the process of swallowing the employment at-will rule, at least in the District of Columbia.

Example

A nurse at a hospital in the District of Columbia testified before the D.C. City Council in favor of patients' rights legislation and a tort reform bill, both of which the hospital opposed. She also served as an expert witness in medical malpractice cases. When the hospital fired her, she sued for wrongful discharge and won at trial. The D.C. Court of Appeals upheld the trial court, ruling that the District's public policy includes the right of an employee to speak out publicly on issues affecting the public interest without fear of retaliation.

Carl v. Children's Hosp., 702 A.2d 159 (D.C.1997)

The wrongful discharge concept continues to be shaped on a case-by-case basis. As the following examples show, it is difficult to predict just what public policies a court will see as important enough to support a suit for wrongful discharge.

Example

A California employer had a rule that prohibited fighting in the workplace and that required employees to avoid physical conflict whenever possible. The rule went so far as to require an employee to retreat—to run from a fight—if he or she could. In an earlier incident, an employee of the company attacked a co-worker without provocation. In a later incident, the employee threatened the same co-worker by swinging a piece of wood at him, then picking up either a hammer or a box of screws and hitting the co-worker with it. The co-worker fled and the threatening employee followed. When they were some 30 or 40 feet apart, the employee threw a box of screws, hitting the co-worker in the back. At that point, the co-worker stopped his retreat, rushed the employee and grabbed him in a bear hug in an attempt to restrain him. In the process, the co-worker was struck on the head and bled profusely.

The employer took the view that co-worker should have continued his retreat and it fired him for violating company policy. The co-worker sued for wrongful discharge, arguing (accurately) that California law gave him a right to defend himself. An intermediate appellate court recognized that California law *permits* an individual to stand and fight, but said that nothing in California law *encourages* him to do so. The court saw no reason why the public interest would be harmed by an employer's requirement that employees must avoid physical conflict in the workplace whenever possible. Therefore, the court upheld the firing.

Escalante v. Wilson's Art Studio, Inc., 135 Cal. Rptr. 2d 187 (2003)

A pair of cases, one from Ohio and the other from Maryland, shows how courts can disagree over the very same issue when it comes to judging whether a particular employer action violates public policy.

Example 1

A psychologist began working for an Ohio organization in 1990. During the course of his employment, a dispute arose between the psychologist and the organization concerning the terms of a life insurance policy that the organization had agreed to obtain. Unable to resolve the dispute to his satisfaction, the psychologist filed suit. His employer responded, first by placing him on administrative leave, and a few weeks later, by firing him. After being terminated, the psychologist amended his suit to add a claim that his firing was abusive.

In rejecting the psychologist's suit, an Ohio appeals court recognized a clear public policy favoring *access to legal representation*. According to the court, *an employee may consult an attorney to determine his rights and remedies under the law.* But actually filing suit is another matter. Employees in that situation have a choice. They may file suit and jeopardize their employment, or they may forego litigation to protect their employment relationship. To rule otherwise, said the court, would disrupt the balance of the employer-employee relationship.

Taylor v. Volunteers of America, 795 N.E.2d 716 (Ohio App. 2003)

Example 2

Deborah worked for a business that provides in-home care to senior citizens. In April 1999, she received a mediocre evaluation. In August of that year, she was issued a written report warning that, absent marked improvement, she would be fired. Deborah's boss required her to sign the report, but Deborah refused to do so, believing it contained intentionally false criticisms of her work. Instead, she took the report home for further review. On a day she was scheduled to be off, Deborah called into work and said she would be consulting with an attorney

(continued)

about the report before responding. Later that day, Deborah's boss called her back and fired her. Deborah sued, claiming that her termination was a wrongful discharge in violation of Maryland public policy. Maryland's highest court ruled that the general right to consult with counsel is not such a sufficiently important public policy to support a wrongful discharge claim.

Porterfield v. Mascari II, Inc., 823 A.2d 590 (Md. 2003)

One consistent theme has emerged from the cases—firing an employee for refusing to commit an illegal act or for fulfilling a duty required by law, is abusive and will provide grounds for a wrongful discharge suit. Another theme is that employees will be protected from termination for exercising rights granted or protected by law.

Things become less clear when the employee is engaged in conduct that is permitted by law, or is even seen as socially desirable, but is not necessarily protected by law. How should an employer proceed in the face of uncertain and changing rules? A prudent employer should hesitate to fire an at-will employee for:

- ◆ engaging in an activity that is protected by law, encouraged by the law, or is usually considered of value to society or
- ◆ refusing to engage in illegal conduct or conduct that is usually considered immoral, improper, or objectionable.

21

The Firing Process

Having a standardized, well thought out procedure for firing employees helps minimize embarrassment to the employee being fired, it reduces the risk of a successful lawsuit, and it helps protect the security of company personnel and resources.

Giving Notice

The procedure should begin with completion of a written *separation notice*, containing at least the following information:

- ◆ the employee's name and Social Security number;
- ◆ the employee's title and usual place of work;
- ◆ the effective date of termination;
- ◆ the reason for the separation (*e.g.*, voluntary quit, lack of work, discharge, or resignation in lieu of discharge);
- ◆ a full explanation of the circumstances of the separation, including grounds for discharging the employee;
- ◆ whether the employee is eligible for rehire;
- ◆ the name and signature of the person completing the form, and the date of completion; and,
- ◆ the name and signature of any other company official whose approval is needed, and the date of approval.

One copy of the form will be placed in the employee's personnel file and another copy will be given to the employee at the meeting when he or she is informed about the termination. In order to facilitate the filing of unemployment insurance claims, some states require employers to furnish a prescribed form of separation notice to all terminated employees. Other states require such a form to be furnished only if the employee requests one.

If the employee is being involuntarily terminated, someone has to tell him or her about the company's decision. That someone needs to pick a time and place to do so and needs to plan what to say. The *who, when, where,* and *what* of firing need to be thought through in advance. Spontaneity is not desirable here. Nor will a pink slip on the employee's desk suffice, because personal involvement is critical to a successful process.

As to *who*, a person senior to the employee with authority to hire and fire should be involved, along with another representative of management. One of them will actually conduct the session and speak for the company. The other will be present as a silent witness as to what is said. Having a second company official present also adds authority to the process and makes it clear to the departing employee that the company's decision is firm. It also discourages a violent or other inappropriate reaction. (The presence of company security guards is even more intimidating, but this approach should only be used if there is genuine reason to fear that the employee will become violent or destructive.)

The *when* and *where* of firing will depend on the circumstances. If the employee has reported to work under the influence of drugs or alcohol, or if the employee has seriously misbehaved (for example, struck a supervisor or maliciously damaged company property), immediate action needs to be taken. Probably the most prudent course here is to suspend the employee and order him or her to leave the company's premises while further discipline is considered in a calmer setting.

What to say? This needs to be carefully scripted. The employee should be told in clear and unambiguous terms that the company is terminating him or her, and should be told a specific date for his or her last day of work. The reason for the termination should be briefly stated as well, although the company official who is doing the firing should not engage in a debate over whether the reason is factually accurate or whether it justifies termination. The reason given should be truthful, without being demeaning or overly critical. *You are being fired for repeated tardiness* is fine. *You are a lazy, incompetent fool* is not. Truthfulness is important because whatever is said here is sure to resurface in any unemployment insurance claim or wrongful discharge suit that follows. A statement such as, *"It is just not working out,"* is no reason at all, and is likely to draw suspicion that the termination is for an illegal reason.

Minimizing Embarrassment and Hardship

Assuming immediate action is not called for, the termination should be timed to cause the least embarrassment and hardship to the employee. It should be done in private, not in front of a roomful of co-workers. It should be done at a time when the fewest number of fellow employees are around, such as late on a Friday afternoon or between shifts. A firing during Christmas week or while the employee is caring for a seriously ill child does not play well to juries. If possible, delay the firing until the holiday or the crisis has passed.

Anticipating Questions

The company official doing the firing should anticipate questions the employee may ask and be ready to respond. Be prepared for questions like the following.

- Is there any chance you will change your mind?
- Can you delay the effective date?
- Will you accept my resignation in lieu of firing me?
- Do I get a severance package?
- When will my final paycheck be issued?

- Will you cash out my accrued leave?
- What about my health insurance?
- What kind of reference will you give me?
- Will you release me from my noncompete agreement?

Not all these questions can be immediately answered. As to the noncompete agreement question, for example, the appropriate response might be, "*You will need to write a letter to the HR Department and someone will get back to you.*"

The firing process itself should be fairly brief. Although the employee may have a lot more questions and may attempt to prolong the session, an extended discussion serves little purpose. There is additional business to accomplish in connection with the employee's departure, but the firing session is not the time or place for it.

Immediately after the session, the company official who did the firing should prepare a draft file memo summarizing the session and the other member of management who was present should review the draft. A final version should then be placed in the employee's personnel file.

Exit Strategies

The employee's immediate reaction to being fired is likely to be denial. But that emotion may quickly lead to anger, resentment, and a desire for revenge. Having seemingly little to lose, an employee in that position can be dangerous in a number of ways. If there is reason to believe the employee may become violent, the employer will want to plan in advance to have security guards on standby. Short of violence, the employer needs to be concerned about the employee's access to company financial resources and electronic data. Depending on the circumstances, the employer may want to take one or more of the following protective steps:

- escort the employee off the company's premises immediately after the firing session;

◆ terminate the employee's signature authority over financial accounts;

◆ change all computer network passwords;

◆ collect keys, electronic access cards, and ID badges;

◆ cancel or collect the employee's company credit cards; and,

◆ inform the employee that he or she is prohibited from returning to the employer's premises and will be considered a trespasser if he or she returns.

In some circumstances, there may be little the employer can do to protect itself from a fired employee's anger.

Example

A disgruntled former employee of a computer chip manufacturer in California sent e-mails to thousands of the company's employees on a number of separate occasions. The company requested the former employee to stop his e-mail barrage, but the former employee refused and took steps to evade company security measures. The company went to court and was awarded an injunction on the basis of an old legal doctrine known as *trespass to chattels*. In June 2003, however, the California Supreme Court threw out the injunction. The court ruled that in order to succeed on a trespass-to-chattels claim, the company would have to show that it suffered or was threatened with some actual damage—either to the computer system itself, or to the company's ability to use the system. Neither was shown in this case.

Intel Corp. v. Hamidi, 1 Cal.Rptr.3d 32 (2003)

Defamation

The firing process can result in claims of *defamation*. To defame someone is to make a false statement of fact that injures the person's reputation. A *written* defamatory statement is *libelous*. A *spoken* defamatory statement is known as *slander*. In order for a person to have a good claim of defamation, the false statement must be *published*—communicated either in writing or orally to some third person. Generally, to be defamatory, the statement must be one of fact, not merely an opinion.

Example

A home furnishings chain in New Mexico had a company policy requiring its employees to fill out a charge slip for any merchandise they were personally buying before removing the merchandise from the store. On at least two occasions, the manager of a particular store removed items without filling out a charge slip. On the second occasion, the manager's supervisor took the manager to a back office and fired him. The two of them then continued to discuss the matter as they left the back office and an argument ensued.

While in the retail area of the store, the supervisor said to the manager—in a loud voice overheard by others—*I don't trust you.* A few months later, the supervisor was asked by another former store employee about the reason the manager was fired. The supervisor's response was, *"He was fired for stealing."* The manager then sued for defamation. The New Mexico Supreme Court ruled that the statement, *I don't trust you* was an expression of opinion, but the second statement, which specifically mentioned stealing, was defamatory.

Newberry v. Allied Stores, Inc., 773 P.2d 1231 (N.M.1989)

Conduct alone can amount to defamation. Suppose that after being informed of his or her termination, an employee is searched by armed security guards and then forcibly removed from the premises, all in front of the employee's co-workers. That conduct could give rise to a good defamation claim as well.

Additional Steps

After the firing process itself is concluded, the employer will want to take these additional steps:

- ◆ collect laptops, cell phones, and other property belonging to the employer;
- ◆ confirm the employee's current address and phone number;
- ◆ instruct the employee to remove all personal belongings;
- ◆ remind the employee of any continuing confidentiality, non-compete, and nonsolicitation agreements he or she may have signed;
- ◆ remind the employee of the employer's policy on references;
- ◆ inform other employees who are directly affected by the termination (without discussing the reason for the termination); and,
- ◆ on a need-to-know basis, inform persons outside the company with whom the employee had contact, such as customers, vendors, financial institutions, and persons receiving garnishment or withholding order payments, about the termination (again, without discussing the reason).

The company may want to develop a standard written checklist of steps to be taken in connection with separations from employment, as well as the dates each step needs to be taken. As each item is accomplished, it should be checked off, dated, and initialed.

A final W-2 form for a terminated employee is not due until the following January 31. However, the employee may request a W-2 sooner than that and the employer then has thirty days to provide it.

22

Final Pay
and Continued Benefits

Once a fired employee's initial anger has subsided, he or she is likely to focus on getting a final paycheck and any accrued but unused leave cashed out. The employee may also be concerned about his or her rights under any benefit plans that survive termination.

Final Pay

A departing employee is entitled to be paid at the agreed rate for all work actually performed up to the time of termination. The employer cannot withhold wages on the ground that the employee failed to give two weeks' or some other specified notice before quitting. Nor can the employer dock the wages of a fired employee on the theory that the employee's work quality was unacceptable.

State law also specifies *when* a departing employee must be paid. In some states, the final paycheck need not be issued until the next regular payday. In other states, the departing employee must be paid immediately or within a few days of termination, depending on the circumstances of termination.

The employer may deduct from the employee's paycheck any claims the employer has against the employee, so long as the employee has *agreed to the deduction in writing*. Suppose, for example, that the employee borrowed money from the company to be repaid out of future paychecks. Or suppose the employer advanced unearned leave on the understanding that, in the event of an early termination, the employee would make reimbursement out of his or her final wages. In these examples, an appropriate setoff against the employee's paycheck is permitted. However, the employer should not deduct the amount of a disputed claim or any other amount not agreed to by the employee, since doing so may violate wage and hour laws.

In most states, annual leave (vacation) is considered part of earned compensation and must be cashed out when an employee quits or is fired. Some states allow employers to adopt a policy of not cashing out accrued but unused leave or limiting the amount that may be carried over (a use-it-or-lose-it policy), but the policy must be clearly communicated to employees *before* they earn the leave.

Example

An association with headquarters in the District of Columbia discharged 80 employees as part of a reduction-in-force. The association paid the discharged employees all salary accrued to the date of separation, plus a severance payment representing up to thirty days (225 hours) of accrued but unused vacation. The association limited the severance payment to thirty days because it had a policy prohibiting employees from accruing more than that amount. A number of former employees who had accrued leave in excess of thirty days brought suit for additional payments.

The court held that, as a general rule, an employee who accrues but does not take paid leave is entitled to be cashed out upon discharge from employment, absent an agreement to the contrary. However, if the employer can show a contrary agreement, then consistent with that agreement the employer need not cash out the leave. To be effective, such agreement need not be a formal countersigned document. It is enough, said the court, if the employer disseminates the policy and the employees elect to stay on the job after learning about the policy.

National Rifle Ass'n v. Ailes, 428 A.2d 816 (D.C. 1981)

Health Insurance Continuation

Employers who have 20 or more employees and who provide group health coverage are subject to the *Consolidated Omnibus Budget Reconciliation Act of 1985* (COBRA). The Act, which requires employers to offer health insurance continuation coverage for most terminated employees, was really a catch-all piece of legislation that just happened to include an amendment to the *Employee Retirement Income Security Act* (ERISA).

Under COBRA, when an employee quits or is involuntarily terminated (except for gross misconduct), the employer must offer him or her the opportunity to continue health coverage at the employee's expense for up to eighteen months. (Termination of employment is known as a *qualifying event* for COBRA purposes. There are other qualifying events that trigger continuation coverage for an employee or his or her family that are not discussed here.)

COBRA contains various deadlines within which notice must be given after the occurrence of a qualifying event. Once on notice that a qualifying event has occurred, the employer must, within 14 days, offer continuing coverage. The employee, spouse, or dependent who is otherwise losing coverage then has 60 days within which to elect COBRA benefits. A notice and reply form follows on pages 200–201.

MODEL COBRA CONTINUATION COVERAGE ELECTION NOTICE
(For use by single-employer group health plans)

[*Enter date of notice*]

Dear: [*Identify the qualified beneficiary(ies), by name or status*]

This notice contains important information about your right to continue your health care coverage in the [*enter name of group health plan*] (the Plan). Please read the information contained in this notice very carefully.

To elect COBRA continuation coverage, follow the instructions on the next page to complete the enclosed Election Form and submit it to us.

If you do not elect COBRA continuation coverage, your coverage under the Plan will end on [*enter date*] due to [*check appropriate box*]:

☐ End of employment   ☐ Reduction in hours of employment
☐ Death of employee   ☐ Divorce or legal separation
☐ Entitlement to Medicare   ☐ Loss of dependent child status

Each person ("qualified beneficiary") in the category(ies) checked below is entitled to elect COBRA continuation coverage, which will continue group health care coverage under the Plan for up to ___ months [*enter 18 or 36, as appropriate and check appropriate box or boxes; names may be added*]:

☐ Employee or former employee
☐ Spouse or former spouse
☐ Dependent child(ren) covered under the Plan on the day before the event that caused
     the loss of coverage
☐ Child who is losing coverage under the Plan because he or she is no
     longer a dependent under the Plan

If elected, COBRA continuation coverage will begin on [*enter date*] and can last until [*enter date*]. [*Add, if appropriate:* You may elect any of the following options for COBRA continuation coverage: [*list available coverage options*].

COBRA continuation coverage will cost: [*enter amount each qualified beneficiary will be required to pay for each option per month of coverage and any other permitted coverage periods.*] You do not have to send any payment with the Election Form. Important additional information about payment for COBRA continuation coverage is included in the pages following the Election Form.

If you have any questions about this notice or your rights to COBRA continuation coverage, you should contact [*enter name of party responsible for COBRA administration for the Plan, with telephone number and address*].

COBRA CONTINUATION COVERAGE ELECTION FORM

INSTRUCTIONS: To elect COBRA continuation coverage, complete this Election Form and return it to us. Under federal law, you must have 60 days after the date of this notice to decide whether you want to elect COBRA continuation coverage under the Plan.

Send completed Election Form to: [*Enter Name and Address*]

This Election Form must be completed and returned by mail [*or describe other means of submission and due date*]. If mailed, it must be post-marked no later than [*enter date*].

If you do not submit a completed Election Form by the due date shown above, you will lose your right to elect COBRA continuation coverage. If you reject COBRA continuation coverage before the due date, you may change your mind as long as you furnish a completed Election Form before the due date. However, if you change your mind after first rejecting COBRA continuation coverage, your COBRA continuation coverage will begin on the date you furnish the completed Election Form.

Read the important information about your rights included in the pages after the Election Form.

I (We) elect COBRA continuation coverage in the [*enter name of plan*] (the Plan) as indicated below:

| Name | Date of Birth | Relationship to Employee | SSN (or other identifier) |

a. _____

    [*Add if appropriate:* Coverage option elected: _____]

b. _____

    [*Add if appropriate:* Coverage option elected: _____]

c. _____

    [*Add if appropriate:* Coverage option elected: _____]

_____   _____

Signature   Date

_____   _____

Print Name   Relationship to individual(s) listed above

_____

_____   _____

Print Address   Telephone number

2

The cost of the continuing benefits must be paid 100% by the employee, even if the employer was paying all or a portion of the premium before the qualifying event. The employer may also charge an additional 2% of the premium to cover its own administrative costs. If the former employee fails to make his or her payments, the employer is free to drop COBRA coverage.

Example

William worked at a factory in Mississippi and was covered by the company's group health insurance plan. When he learned he had cancer, he immediately quit his job. The company then notified him that he had 60 days to elect COBRA continuation coverage, but William responded that he had no income and was unable to pay the premiums, so the company dropped his coverage. In William's later suit for insurance benefits, a federal trial court said that group health plans have the right to require payment for continuation coverage. Under the statute, COBRA rights end on the date on which coverage ceases for failure to make timely payment of any premium. In other words, said the court, those seeking COBRA continuation coverage are not entitled to a free ride.

Butler v. Trustmark Ins. Co., 211 F. Supp. 2d 803 (S.D.Miss. 2002)

(For more information about COBRA, go to **www.dol.gov/dol/topic/health-plans/cobra.htm.**)

Many states have *little COBRA laws* that apply to employers who do not meet the twenty-employee threshold under federal law.

Health Insurance Portability

The federal *Health Insurance Portability and Accountability Act* (HIPAA) imposes a variety of requirements on group health plans in order to make health coverage more *portable*. This way when an employee changes jobs, he or she will more quickly qualify for full coverage from the new employer. For example, HIPAA limits the time period for which preexisting conditions may be excluded to twelve months. The twelve-month limit is further reduced by the employee's *creditable coverage*, meaning coverage under a prior individual policy, under a prior group policy, under COBRA continuation benefits, or under Medicare or Medicaid.

To enable an employee to prove prior coverage, the previous employer or insurer must issue a Certificate of Credible Coverage containing information about the prior plan and the employee's participation. Unlike COBRA, which applies to employers with twenty or more employees, HIPAA applies to all employers who have group health plans. (On the following page is a sample certificate indicating HIPAA coverage.)

HIPAA CERTIFICATE OF COVERAGE

IMPORTANT - This certificate provides evidence of your prior health coverage. You may need to furnish this certificate if you become eligible under a group health plan that excludes coverage for certain medical conditions that you have before you enroll. This certificate may need to be provided if medical advice, diagnosis, care, or treatment was recommended or received for the condition within the 6-month period prior to your enrollment in the new plan. If you become covered under another group health plan, check with the plan administrator to see if you need to provide this certificate. You may also need this certificate to buy, for yourself or your family, an insurance policy that does not exclude coverage for medical conditions that are present before you enroll.

1.   Date of this certificate:

2.   Name of group health plan:

3.   Name of participant:

4.   Identification number of participant:

5.   Names of any dependents to whom this certificate applies:

6.   The name, address and telephone number of the plan administrator or issuer responsible for providing this certificate is:

7.   For further information call:

8.   If the individual(s) identified in line 3 and line 5 has at least 18 months of creditable coverage (disregarding periods of coverage before a 63-day break), check here ____ and skip lines 9 and 10.

9.   Date waiting period or affiliation period (if any) began:

10. Date coverage began:

11. Date coverage ended: _____ (or check if coverage is continuing as of the date of this certificate: _____.

Authorized signature:

Typed or printed name:

Title:

(Additional information about HIPAA is available at **www.dol.gov/ebsa/ faqs/faq_consumer_hipaa.html#.**)

Retirement Plans

Employers need to alert plan administrators about a termination and be sure that all plan requirements are satisfied. Some retirement plans, such as 403(b) annuity plans maintained by tax-exempt nonprofit organizations, are 100% vested and may be unaffected by the termination. Other plans, such as defined benefit plans, may be partially or fully vested but effectively frozen until the former employee reaches retirement age. Defined contributions plans may permit the former employee to take a taxable distribution or to roll over the account balance into in Individual Retirement Account (IRA).

23

Severance Packages and Releases

Employment contracts, particularly those with high-level executives, may specify that, upon termination, the employee is entitled to a severance payment. An employer may also have a standard severance policy spelled out in its employee handbook.

In the absence of an express or implied contract, employers are under no obligation to offer severance to departing employees, even those who have worked loyally for many years or who are being terminated for lack of work. However, sometimes a severance package or some other benefit of value may be just the way to avoid a costly lawsuit.

Example

An employee of a fitness club in New York City was diagnosed with breast cancer in October 2000, after having been on the job for about six months. She underwent surgery and chemotherapy treatment beginning in December and continuing through May of 2001. She was originally scheduled for reconstructive surgery on September 11, 2001, but the events of that day caused a postponement to November. On October 1, 2001, the employee was fired. Arguably, the termination violated the *Americans with Disabilities Act* and the *Family and Medical Leave Act*. Sometime later the club sent her a notice of rights under

(continued)

COBRA to continue her group health insurance.

At the same time, the club offered to pay the first six months of her COBRA premium in exchange for a general release of all claims relating to her employment. (Normally, a departing employee must pay his or her own COBRA premiums, plus a 2% fee to cover the employer's administrative costs.) Eventually, the employee signed the release, but later she apparently had a change of heart and sued the club, alleging violations of the ADA and the FMLA. The court dismissed her claims on the basis that she had voluntarily given up any right to sue, observing that an employee may waive employment discrimination claims as long as the waiver is made knowingly and voluntarily and is supported by adequate consideration—something of value passing to the employee in exchange for the waiver. Here, all the circumstances pointed to a knowing and voluntary waiver, and the consideration—payment of COBRA premiums—was certainly adequate.

Knoll v. Equinox Fitness Clubs, 2003 WL 23018807 (S.D.N.Y. 2003)

One point to note about this example is that, to be effective at all, a release needs to be supported by *consideration*. This could take the form of a cash payment to the employee or something else of value. As in the example, companies who are subject to COBRA may offer to pay for the employee's continuation coverage rather than have the employee pay the on-going premiums. But if a departing employee receives nothing of value for the release, the release will be unenforceable.

Contents of Release

A release is a type of contract by which one party gives up a legal right or claim in exchange for valuable consideration. The valuable consideration is usually cash or some close equivalent. In general, no special form of contract is required to release most types of claims, including discrimination claims.

A release should cover at least the following points.

- ◆ It should specify what the employee is getting as consideration.
- ◆ It should state how any cash payments to the employee will be treated for income tax and withholding purposes.
- ◆ It should be as broad as possible, releasing the whole array of employment-related claims that might arise.
- ◆ It should contain a promise not to sue the employer in court or to initiate arbitration proceedings, and to dismiss any suits or arbitration proceedings then pending against the employer.
- ◆ It should contain a promise not to seek or accept any individualized remedies or benefits that might be awarded as a result of an administrative charge or in a class action.
- ◆ It should contain a promise not to reapply for employment.

Several courts have held that a release provision waiving the employee's right to file charges with the EEOC is void and unenforceable. The *Age Discrimination in Employment Act* (ADEA) now makes that view explicit as to age discrimination claims, saying that no waiver may be used to justify interfering with the protected right of an employee to file a charge or participate in an investigation or proceeding conducted by the EEOC. Even asking an employee to sign such a waiver may constitute illegal discrimination.

Age Discrimination Claims

While no special form of release is required in most cases, the release of an ADEA claim will be ineffective unless the employer follows very specific procedures spelled out in the law. For example, the employee must be advised in writing to consult with an attorney before signing the release. The employee must also be given at least twenty-one days to consider the release before signing it, and an additional seven-day rescission period after signing it to change his or her mind. The law does not require the employee to actually wait twenty-one days before signing the release. The employee can sign earlier, as long as his or her right to take a full twenty-one days is not restricted. On the other hand, the seven-day period after signing cannot be shortened.

The Supreme Court has ruled that where a release did not comply with ADEA requirements, an employee who received severance pay in exchange for a release of his or her ADEA claim was entitled to keep the severance pay and still sue his or her employer for age discrimination. Therefore, an employer who has required a release of all claims in exchange for a severance package should not begin making severance payments to a 40-and-over employee until the seven-day rescission period has expired.

If a release of ADEA claims is requested in connection with an exit incentive or other employment termination program offered to a group or class of employees, the twenty-one day period increases to forty-five days. In addition, the employer must provide all persons in the class or group with:

- a description of the class or group;
- the job titles and ages of all employees eligible or selected for the program; and,
- the ages of all employees in the same job classification or organizational unit who are not eligible or selected for the program.

Wage Disputes

Disputes can sometimes arise over the amount of compensation due to an employee. A salesperson may claim, for example, that he or she is entitled to the commission on a sale, even though the salesperson was terminated before the customer actually made payment under the purchase order. The employer responds that under established company policy, commissions are not paid if the employee quits or is terminated before the customer makes payment. The parties then reach a compromise and exchange a partial commission payment for a written and signed release of claims. A release in that example is binding on the salesperson and provides the employer with a good defense, should the salesperson later sue for the balance of the commission. However, when the dispute involves compensation that is governed by the *Fair Labor Standards Act* (FLSA), a compromise and release reached privately between employer and employee may not be enforceable.

Under the FLSA, employers generally owe time-and-a-half for overtime (time in excess of forty hours per week) to their nonexempt employees. If the employer underpays overtime, the employee may recover not only the balance due but also additional liquidated damages equal to the unpaid amount and the attorneys' fees he or she incurred in pursuing the claim. According to a 1945 Supreme Court decision, unless the settlement agreement provides for payment of all amounts that are clearly due (including liquidated damages), the employee can still sue for the remaining amount to which he or she is entitled according to the FLSA. If there is a *legitimate factual dispute* over how many overtime hours the employee actually worked, then a release in exchange for a compromise payment may be valid, but the question remains open at this writing.

In cases of FLSA wage disputes, one solution is to ask the U.S. Department of Labor to participate in and supervise any settlement that the parties may be able to reach. Prudent employers will want to do just that, particularly if substantial amounts are involved or a whole class of employees claims to have been underpaid.

Taxability of Severance Payments

It has long been the rule that the proceeds of a *personal injury action* (a suit claiming injury to the body or person of the plaintiff) are excluded from taxation and from any withholding or reporting requirements. In the past, the parties to an employment dispute often characterized payments in settlement of the dispute as damages for emotional distress, for injury to reputation, etc. to avoid tax obligations. In 1996, the Internal Revenue Code was amended to narrow the exclusion. The Code now states that gross income does not include damages received on account of personal *physical injuries or physical sickness*. A private letter ruling by the IRS defines personal physical injuries for these purposes as *direct unwanted or uninvited physical contacts resulting in observable bodily harms, such as bruises, cuts, swelling, and bleeding*.

As a result of the 1996 amendment, most payments in employment dispute situations will be included in the employee's gross income for federal income tax purposes. (At the same time, the payments will be deductible by the employer.) In addition, since damages in an employment dispute are usually based on lost wages, the payments are generally viewed as the equivalent of employee compensation, and therefore subject to withholding and reporting requirements.

When an employer agrees to settle an employment dispute or agrees to a severance payment in the face of a potential claim, the agreement should state that the payments are subject to withholding and reporting. If the agreement attempts to characterize any portion of the payment as nontaxable and not subject to withholding or reporting (a risky arrangement), the agreement should at least contain a provision requiring the recipient to indemnify the employer should the IRS later recharacterize the payment as taxable.

If the former employee has been represented by an attorney in connection with negotiating a severance or settlement, a further question arises over the taxability of any amount attributed to the attorney's fee. Many workplace laws provide for payment of the employee's attorney's fees in the event of a successful suit by the employee. During settlement negotiations, the employee's attorney is therefore likely to ask the employer for a contribution toward his or her fee. Even if the parties do not agree to such a contribution, the attorney may ask that whatever fee he or she is due out of the overall settlement (typically a contingent fee based on a percentage of the settlement) be paid directly to him or her by separate check. How should the employer treat this attorney's fee portion for tax reporting purposes?

The IRS takes the position—supported by most courts that have considered the question—that the entire amount, including any portion attributable to the attorney's fee, is taxable income to the former employee. (The attorney must, of course, pay tax on any fees he or she receives, regardless of whether those fees are also considered taxable income to the former employee.) The employee, in turn, may be able to take a miscellaneous deduction for any payments made to the attorney, but the deduction is subject to limitations under the tax code. The result is often that employees pay income tax on amounts they never even receive, or at least on amounts they receive but are obligated to remit to their attorney. As of this writing, the issue is pending before the Supreme Court.

Effect on Unemployment Insurance

To be eligible for benefits, an individual must be *unemployed* during the particular week for which he or she is claiming benefits. A common provision in state unemployment insurance statutes says that an individual is *deemed unemployed in any week with respect to which no wages are payable to the individual and during which the individual performs no services.* Under statutes using definitions such as this, severance payments usually have no effect on eligibility for benefits.

Example

The work of a long-time employee at a company in Illinois had become unsatisfactory and the company opened discussions about the employee's future. Eventually, the company offered and the employee agreed to a lump sum separation payment based on 36 weeks of regular salary. At the employee's request, the payment was spread over two installments in December and January to reduce income taxes. During the period of the separation payments, the employee performed no services for the company. After leaving the company, the employee applied for unem-

(continued)

213

ployment insurance benefits. The Illinois Supreme Court ruled that he was entitled to those benefits because the separation payments were made with respect to prior services, not with respect to services performed during the payment period.

Kroger Co. v. Blumenthal, 148 N.E.2d 734 (Ill. 1958)

However, in some states, a severance package that is paid out over time or that is based on the amount of the former employee's compensation and benefits makes the discharged employee ineligible for unemployment insurance. In those states, the employer will want to design its separation payments so that the former employee cannot collect benefits on top of the severance package.

24

References

To give or not to give a reference? If you decide to give a reference and you include some negative information about your former employee, he or she may sue you for defamation. (see Chapter 21.) If you omit the negative information and your former employee gets hired on the strength of your recommendation, you may be sued for any losses caused by your former employee's subsequent misconduct.

Example

An administrator at a junior high school in California had inappropriate sexual contact with girls at the school on a number of occasions. Despite school officials' awareness of this, they gave him a recommendation letter that stressed positive aspects of his work, describing him as an upbeat, enthusiastic administrator who related well to the students and who was largely responsible for providing a safe, orderly, and clean environment for students and staff. The letter did not mention anything negative. Helped by this recommendation, the administrator was able to obtain a job at a new school, where he sexually assaulted a student. The student's mother sued the first school, claiming that the recommendation letter was negligent and that the first school should be held liable for the student's injuries. The California Supreme Court agreed and ruled for the mother.

Randi W. v. Muroc Joint Unified School Dist., 60 Cal. Rptr. 2d 263 (Cal.1997)

The safest course is not to give any reference at all or to give what some call a *neutral* or *no-comment reference*, which only confirms employment without including any evaluation. While many employers have adopted this approach, they do so at great social cost. Employees who should be rejected get hired because former employers will not give a candid evaluation. At the same time, quality employees who *should* be hired get passed over because their prior accomplishments never surface.

Privilege

An employer's policy of giving substantive references is not completely foolhardy. A statement that might otherwise be defamatory can sometimes be *privileged*—protected by law from a claim of defamation—even though the statement is false, conveyed to a third person, and is injurious to reputation. In this context, privileges are either *absolute* or they are *conditional* (sometimes called *qualified*). An absolute privilege is a complete bar to a claim of defamation. It is the type of privilege members of Congress enjoy when they give speeches on the floor of the House of Representatives.

The courts in most states have concluded that an employer's reference, even if it contains a factually false and damaging statement, is protected under the so-called *common interest privilege*. Courts have defined the common interest privilege as covering communications made in good faith between parties who have a common interest in the subject matter of the communication. This includes, for example, a former employer and a prospective new employer, who both have an interest in determining whether an individual is a qualified employee. The common interest privilege, however, is only *conditional*. This means it can be lost if:

- it is made without any legitimate business purpose;
- it is made with knowledge of its falsity or with a reckless disregard for its truth or falsity;

- it is made with malice, spite, or ill will toward the employee; or,
- the employer disseminates the statement beyond those who have a business-related need to know.

> **Example**
>
> An employee at a Tennessee hospital was discharged for obtaining and cashing other employees' payroll checks. She sued for defamation, claiming that the hospital told other employees about her alleged misconduct. A Tennessee appeals court ruled that since the statements were confined to hospital personnel only and were made during the course of an investigation, there was no publication of the statements to any outside third parties. In addition, even if internal dissemination amounted to publication, the statements were conditionally privileged.
>
> *Tate v. Baptist Memorial Hosp., 2000 WL 1051851 (Tenn.App. 2000)*

A few states have adopted laws extending statutory protection to employers who give substantive references, unless they intentionally give false reference information or act maliciously without any legitimate business reason.

In addition to privilege protection, employers who give substantive references can gain some additional protection by insisting that any employee who wants a reference must first give the employer a written release of claims or must approve the specific wording of the reference.

Whatever policy you adopt, be sure it is communicated to all employees and that it is faithfully followed. The policy should also identify those persons within the company who are authorized to give out reference information and it should prohibit everyone else within the company from doing so.

Compelled Self-Publication

In a few states, even a no-comment policy does not provide complete protection. Under a doctrine known as *compelled self-publication*, the courts recognize that since the employee must honestly tell a prospective employer about the reason given for his or her termination, the employee has no choice but to defame him- or herself. Therefore, he or she may sue the former employer for defamation.

Example

A Minnesota-based health insurance company hired four individuals to work as dental claims approvers. After some six months on the job, they were temporarily sent from the insurer's office in St. Paul to the company's Pittsburgh office to help clear out a claims backlog. None of them had ever traveled on company business before and none of them were familiar with the company's expense reporting requirements. After they returned to St. Paul, they were told for the first time they would have to submit expense reports and were instructed on the procedure. After reconstructing their expenses as best they could and submitting their reports, they were furnished with different reporting guidelines and told to resubmit their reports. Subsequently, they were given yet another set of guidelines and told to make further changes. At this point, the four employees balked, saying they would stand by their original submissions, which showed their actual and reasonable expenses.

The company then fired them for gross insubordination. When the individuals looked for new jobs, they were asked about the circumstances of their prior separations. In each case, they honestly said the reason they were given was gross insubordination. (The insurer itself had a no-comment reference policy and never told anyone outside the company about the firings.) All four found it difficult to secure new

(continued)

> employment and they suffered financial hardship as a result. In their lawsuit for defamation, the Minnesota Supreme Court ruled that even though the company did not itself publish the false statement, it should have foreseen the employees involved would be under strong compulsion to repeat the statement to prospective employers. The court therefore upheld their defamation claims.
>
> *Lewis v. Equitable Life Assur. Soc. of the U.S.*, 389 N.W.2d 876 (Minn.1986)

Fortunately, most courts that have considered the question have rejected the doctrine of compelled self-publication.

Discrimination against Former Employees

Employment discrimination laws protect existing employees, making it illegal to take an adverse employment action on the basis of race, sex, etc. Employers also need to be aware that *former* employees also enjoy protection in a variety of ways.

In a 1997 Supreme Court case of *Robinson v. Shell Oil Co.*, an oil company employee filed a charge of race discrimination with the EEOC after he was fired. While that charge was pending, the employee applied for work with another employer, who in turn contacted the oil company for a reference. Claiming that the oil company gave him a negative reference because he had filed the EEOC charge, the employee filed an additional charge of retaliation. The oil company defended the retaliation charge on the basis that *Title VII* of the *Civil Rights Act* only covers existing employees and candidates for employment, not former employees. A unanimous Supreme Court disagreed, ruling that the term *employee* as used in the law should, in appropriate contexts, be read to include a former employee.

25

Enforcing Restrictive Covenants

You have learned that your former employee is now working for the competition in violation of a noncompete agreement, is using confidential information, or is soliciting customers and fellow employees for his or her new business. Your first step should be to consult with experienced employment law counsel to evaluate the strength of your legal position and plan strategy. The advice you are likely to receive at this point is to write to your former employee, remind your former employee of his or her contractual obligations, and demand that he or she *cease and desist* violating those obligations.

If the former employee is now working for a competitor, your legal counsel will also probably advise that a letter be written to the successor employer, informing the employer about the restrictive covenant and insisting that it not participate in the employee's breach of the agreement. This is often the simplest and cheapest means of enforcing the agreement. It works because the successor employer, once on notice of the agreement, can be sued for *tortious interference with contract* if it ignores the agreement and continues to enjoy the benefits of the former employee's breach of contract.

Example

A biomedical engineer worked for a Minnesota manufacturing company making cardiovascular medical devices. During his employment, he became one of the company's top scientists with access to highly confidential company information. As a result of his position, he was required to sign a noncompete agreement that prohibited his working for a competitor for one year after his employment ended. In return, the company promised that if the noncompete agreement restricted his ability to earn a comparable salary, the company would supplement his income.

After sixteen years on the job, the engineer resigned and went to work for a direct competitor, despite having been reminded that working for the competitor would violate the agreement. The competitor itself was aware of the noncompete agreement when it hired the engineer. So the company sued the engineer for breach of the agreement and it sued the competitor for tortious interference with contract. The Minnesota Supreme Court agreed that the engineer had breached the noncompete agreement. The Court also allowed the company to recover almost $100,000 in damages against the competitor, representing the attorney fees and expenses the company had incurred in enforcing its noncompete agreement against the engineer.

Kallok v. Medtronics, Inc., 573 N.W.2d 356 (Minn. 1998)

Even if the employee does not immediately cease and desist, your letters may lead to discussions of an acceptable three-way settlement among you, your former employee, and his or her new employer. For example, there may be just a handful of customers that you really care about and you may be able to extract an agreement to leave those customers alone. The new employer may be willing to reassign your former employee to a position that does not involve direct competition. Or perhaps you would be happy to give up your breach-of-contract claim for a cash payment.

If your letters do not produce a satisfactory result, your next step will probably be filing a lawsuit and asking the court for an *injunction*. An injunction is a court order prohibiting specified conduct, such as working for the competition or disclosing confidential information. A violation of such a court order can result in fines or jail time.

Injunction litigation is usually over fairly quickly, but it is intense, expensive, and disruptive. As with any litigation, you will want to weigh the costs against the damage your former employee is causing you and the likelihood you will prevail in a suit against him or her. You will have the burden of proving that your restrictive covenant is reasonable and that you need an injunction to prevent unfair competition. You must also overcome the court's natural reluctance to grant injunctions, both because they are considered extraordinary remedies and because they may have the effect of putting your former employee out of work.

An injunction cannot, of course, require your employee to continue working for you, since the U.S. Constitution and federal law prohibit contracts of *involuntary servitude*.

An alternative to an injunction might be to sue your employee for money damages caused by his or her contract breach. This is usually not practical, since it is difficult to quantify the loss you are suffering as a result of your employee's working for a competitor, and since the law will not award *speculative damages*. There may be situations, however, where you can show that a long-standing customer who regularly generates a steady stream of revenue left as a result of your former employee's breach and now sends its business to your competitor.

If your company is in Illinois, North Carolina, or a few other states, you may be able to get an injunction even if you did not have the foresight to get a restrictive covenant from your employee. The courts in these states have adopted a legal doctrine known as *inevitable disclosure*. Under that doctrine, even when there is no actual or threatened disclosure of trade secrets, the court may enjoin a former employee from working with the competition:

- if the former employee had access to highly confidential, specifically identified trade secrets;
- if the employee's old and new companies are in direct competition; and,
- if the employee's old and new jobs are so similar as to make disclosure of the secrets inevitable.

The courts in most other states, however, will not grant injunctions on the basis of the inevitable disclosure doctrine.

One other possible remedy for unfair competition deserves mention. In the absence of a noncompete agreement, you will not be able to enjoin a departing employee's right to compete *after* he or she leaves you, but you may be able to sue for damages if the competition began *before* the departure. All employees—even at-will employees who have not signed noncompete agreements—owe a duty of loyalty to their employers. This means, for example, that while employees may make plans to compete once they have quit and gone out on their own, employees cannot actually engage in competition while still employed.

Example

The employer in this case was in the business of repairing and maintaining sewer and storm water pipes in Hawaii. Two of the company's laborers, while still employed by the company, formed their own partnership and successfully bid against the company on a local government project. When the company learned of their disloyalty, it fired them. Apparently undaunted by being fired, the two employees sued for overtime wages they claimed were due. The company countersued. At

(continued)

trial, the court dismissed the employees' overtime claim, and it ruled that the employees had to disgorge the profits they had made competing against the company. In addition, the trial court ordered the employees to pay interest on those profits, and it required the employees to reimburse the company for its attorney fees. It made no difference that the two employees here were only low-level. The duty of loyalty, said the court, applies to all employees, not just officers and directors.

Eckard Brandes, Inc. v. Riley, 338 F.3d 1082 (9th Cir. 2003)

26

Unemployment Insurance

The unemployment insurance system is a cooperative arrangement between the federal government and state governments to pay temporary benefits to persons who are *out of work involuntarily*. In essence, the federal government provides certain administrative functions, while state governments fund the payment of benefits. The system is financed through mandatory taxes (called *contributions*) imposed on covered employers by state unemployment insurance laws, and at the federal level, by the *Federal Unemployment Tax Act* (FUTA).

Employers who have been in business for more than three or four years pay contributions at an *earned rate* that is based in part on the employer's actual claims experience. Because of the experience factor, hiring and firing practices can have a significant impact on the amount of future unemployment tax due. The more employees that are laid off, the more claims that are likely to be filed and the higher the employer's future contributions will be.

Tax-exempt organizations may have the option under state law of making reimbursements for benefits charged against their account instead of making contributions in advance. Electing to reimburse may improve a charity's current cash flow, but it could prove highly expensive in the event several employees are terminated at the same time.

Misconduct and Quitting without Good Cause

At the heart of unemployment insurance is the requirement that the person claiming benefits be out of work *involuntarily*, through no fault of his or her own. An individual who is fired for misconduct is therefore disqualified from receiving benefits. Some states have gradations of misconduct, such as *aggravated misconduct*, *gross misconduct*, and *plain misconduct*. In states with gradations of misconduct, the most serious level may disqualify the employee from benefits entirely, whereas lesser degrees of misconduct may result in only temporary disqualification.

If an employee is discharged for misconduct and the employer decides to contest (*controvert*) the payment of benefits, the employer normally must prove:

- that the employer had a clear, well-established work rule;
- that the employee knew about the work rule; and,
- that the employee willfully violated the work rule.

Proving the first two points should be relatively easy if the employer has an employee handbook and requires each employee to sign a receipt acknowledging that he or she has been given a copy and is expected to be familiar with its contents.

Example

A nationwide car rental company entered into a *collective bargaining agreement* (CBA) with its driver-employees. The CBA required each employee to maintain a valid drivers license and to report immediately to the company any suspension or revocation of his or her license. The CBA specified that failure to do so would result in immediate termination. When one of the company's Illinois employees failed to report his license suspension after receiving a number of traffic tickets, he was

(continued)

> fired. In his subsequent claim for unemployment insurance benefits, the employer disputed benefits on the basis of misconduct. The employee countered that he knew about the reporting requirement, but he did not know his license had been suspended. (The notice of suspension was apparently mailed to an old address.) An Illinois appeals court ruled that there was no misconduct because the employee had not deliberately violated company rules. However, the employee was solely responsible for his becoming disqualified to hold the driving job and therefore, he was ineligible for benefits.
>
> *Horton v. Department of Employment Security, 781 N.E.2d 545 (Ill.App. 2002)*

Normally, if an employee voluntarily quits, he or she is not entitled to benefits either. But unemployment insurance statutes usually specify that the disqualification only applies if the employee leaves work *without good cause*. Stated another way, if an employee voluntarily quits *with* good cause, he or she is not disqualified and may receive benefits.

To constitute good cause, the reason for quitting must be connected in some way to the job the employee is leaving, such as intolerable working conditions or delayed pay checks. A purely personal decision by the employee will not qualify. For example, leaving to take a better job, to become self-employed, to return to school, or to relocate with a spouse are not good causes.

Example

Valerie worked as a checker in a South Dakota grocery store. After a bank deposit was discovered missing, store management asked the local police department to interview all employees. Valerie was among those interviewed. Attempting to force a confession, police officials informed Valerie that they believed she was the thief, that if she admitted taking the money she could keep her job, but if she did not, she would

(continued)

lose her job and her children would be taken away from her. At that point, Valerie stated that in her opinion the whole procedure was "bull" and she left.

The next day, when Valerie did not report to work, store management contacted her and asked her to come in to talk further. When she complied, management repeated the accusation that she was the guilty one and that if she left without admitting guilt, her employer did not ever want to see her face again. Valerie continued to deny involvement and she left, believing she had been fired. When she subsequently applied for unemployment insurance benefits, her employer controverted her claim on the basis that she had voluntarily left her job without good cause and was therefore disqualified.

The South Dakota Supreme Court sided with Valerie. It pointed out that under state law, an employee has good cause for leaving a job if the employer's conduct demonstrates a substantial disregard of the standards of behavior that an employee has a right to expect. In this case, absent any evidence of Valerie's guilt, a demand that she admit guilt to retain her job fell below standards of conduct that an employee has a right to expect. Therefore, Valerie quit with good cause and she was entitled to collect unemployment.

Habben v. G. F. Buche, Co., 677 N.W.2d 227 (S.D. 2004)

Strikes

Is an employee who is on strike considered to be out of work voluntarily or involuntarily for unemployment insurance purposes? In general, benefits are denied to employees who are out of work because of a labor dispute at their worksite. However, a claimant is generally *not* disqualified despite the existence of a labor dispute at his or her worksite if the claimant is not personally involved in the labor dispute and if the claimant does not belong to a grade or class of workers whose members are involved in the labor dispute.

An individual who is receiving benefits may turn down a job that has become vacant because of a strike and still continue to receive benefits. Unemployment laws do not force workers to become strikebreakers.

Claim Procedure

An individual who loses his or her job must register for work and file a claim with the appropriate state agency. When the state agency receives a claim, it notifies the claimant's prior employers. The employer must then submit *separation information* to the state agency, giving the reason why the employment terminated, the last day of employment, the claimant's wage rate, and other information that might affect eligibility for or the amount of benefits. Providing false information in order to disqualify a claimant is criminal. Once the state agency makes an initial determination of entitlement to benefits, the employer may contest benefits by appealing the determination to a hearing examiner.

One obvious reason for an employer to contest benefits (assuming there are reasonable grounds to do so) is to protect the employer's earned rate. A less obvious reason to contest a claim is to get a preview of any related claims the former employee may intend to bring against the employer. Suppose, for example, that the employee voluntarily quit but says in his or her claim for unemployment benefits that he or she had good cause to leave due to racial discrimination on the job. Or suppose the employee says he or she was fired for refusal to perform some illegal act, such as lying to a safety inspector. In those circumstances, the employer can reasonably expect to be faced not only with an unemployment compensation claim, but also with a charge of discrimination or a suit for abusive discharge.

If benefits are contested, the state unemployment agency must conduct a hearing at which the employee may testify, call other witnesses, and present documents. The employer, usually with the assistance of its attorney, can cross-examine the employee and his or her witnesses and can examine documentary evidence. The opportunity to do so at this stage is particularly valuable. Employees may not be fully prepared, they may not be represented by counsel, and they could make statements that will prove harmful to later claims.

> ### Example
>
> An employee for a New York company left the company and filed a claim for unemployment insurance benefits. The claim was denied after a hearing on the basis that he had voluntarily left employment without good cause. The employee then sued the company for wrongful discharge, claiming that he left for fear of his own safety. The court dismissed the employee's wrongful discharge suit, ruling that in the earlier unemployment insurance hearing, the employee had raised and lost the issue of good cause for leaving and was barred from relitigating that same issue in his wrongful discharge suit.
>
> *Shaffer v. Victory Van Lines, Inc., 697 N.Y.S.2d 166 (App.Div. 1999)*

Trade Adjustment Assistance

When workers in a particular industry are adversely affected by an increase in imports of foreign goods, the *Trade Act of 1974* allows them, their unions, or their employers to petition the Secretary of Labor for a determination that the workers are eligible for *trade adjustment assistance* (TAA). This assistance is basically a continuation of unemployment insurance benefits once regular benefits have run out.

Recent amendments to the Trade Act entitle TAA-eligible workers to a second chance to elect COBRA as well. Workers who, for whatever reason, did not elect COBRA coverage following the original qualifying event (job loss) have an additional sixty days following their becoming TAA-eligible to elect COBRA coverage. This second chance election must be made within six months after the original, TAA-related loss of health insurance.

The new law does not specify what, if any, duty the employer has to notify workers of their second chance election. Presumably, this will be clarified in Department of Labor regulations. The new law does say that after a second chance election, coverage commences at the beginning of the new 60-day election period. In other words, coverage does not reach all the way back to the original qualifying event. It is not clear whether COBRA continuation coverage—which typically lasts up to eighteen months following a job loss—runs from the original qualifying event or from the effective date of the second chance election.

The *Health Insurance Portability and Accountability Act* (HIPAA) is also affected. The new law says that if second chance COBRA coverage is elected, the period between the original, TAA-related loss of coverage and the commencement of second chance COBRA coverage does not constitute a break in coverage for preexisting condition computation purposes.

Conclusion

The beginning of a new employment relationship, much like any other relationship, brings much excitement and a sense that this one will be perfect. But employees—and employers, for that matter—are never perfect. So when the imperfections surface, disappointment may follow.

The path from excitement to disappointment may be inevitable in some relationships, but it need not necessarily be followed when it comes to employment. A carefully planned hiring process allows for the exchange of all relevant information, so that the minuses as well as the pluses are apparent and can be evaluated at the outset. Candor, or at least the avoidance of outright deception, is essential.

The parties also need to be candid with themselves. Employers must develop a clear picture of the job being advertised and the skills needed. Employees must realistically appraise their own abilities and the extent to which a particular job offers a genuine opportunity for success and satisfaction. Only then will both parties be able to make a fair assessment of each other and reach informed decisions about whether to offer and accept a position.

Open communication during the relationship will enable the parties to understand their respective expectations, to meet those expectations if possible, and to adjust them when necessary. Should it eventually become clear that the relationship is not working, neither party will be unduly surprised.

A decision to end a failing relationship is not easily made, but when it clearly needs to be made, further delay is inevitably destructive. Here again, directness and candor are the best tools.

With this book as your guide, you should now be able to traverse the workplace minefield, from hiring to firing, relatively unscathed.

Glossary

A

abusive discharge. Sometimes called wrongful discharge, the termination of an at-will employee for engaging in protected activity or for refusing to commit an illegal act.

affirmative action. Action, required of most government contractors and subcontractors, to assure equal employment of minorities, women, persons with disabilities, and certain veterans.

Age Discrimination in Employment Act (ADEA). The ADEA prohibits discrimination because of age against persons forty or more years old.

agent. A person who acts on behalf of another (called the principal), who has the power to bind the other person in contract. Employees and independent contractors can each be, but are not necessarily, agents of their employers.

agency shop. A type of union security arrangement where union membership is optional, but as a condition of continued employment, nonunion members pay to the union amounts equal to initiation fees and periodic dues paid by union members.

alternative dispute resolution (ADR). A procedure for resolving disputes other than by a lawsuit. Arbitration, mediation, and conciliation are forms of ADR.

Americans with Disabilities Act (ADA). The ADA prohibits discrimination against a qualified person with a disability and requires reasonable accommodation of disabled applicants and employees.

arbitration. One of several forms of dispute resolution that are alternatives to litigation in court.

at-will employment. Employment that is not for any fixed or definite term. In an at-will employment relationship, the employee can quit at any time and the employer can fire the employee at any time with or without cause.

B

backpay. Pay awarded to an employee or applicant for employment that, but for discrimination, an unfair labor practice, or other wrongful conduct by the employer, would have been earned between the time of the wrongful conduct and the time the award is made.

blacklisting. The practice of circulating the names of former employees who should not be hired because of their history of union organizing efforts or other protected activity.

***bona fide* occupational qualification (BFOQ).** Exceptions to certain forms of discrimination.

borrowed servant. An employee who is transferred from his or her regular employer to another employer on a temporary basis.

C

casual employee. An employee who is not covered by workers' compensation because he or she works irregularly, for a brief period only, doing work not normally performed by employees of the employer.

cause. A reason that is legally sufficient to discharge an employee who has an employment contract.

child labor. Labor by a person under 18 years-of-age.

Circular E. An IRS publication for employers, also known as Publication 15, containing instructions and tables for federal income tax withholding and payroll tax obligations.

Civil Rights Act. The Act, which was significantly amended in 1991, is the principal federal statute prohibiting discrimination in employment and public accommodations. *Title VII* is the portion of the *Civil Rights Act* dealing with employment discrimination.

closed shop. A type of union security agreement where employees must be union members in order to be hired.

COBRA (Consolidated Omnibus Budget Reconciliation Act). COBRA requires continuation of group health insurance coverage under certain circumstances when coverage would otherwise end.

collective bargaining agreement (CBA). An agreement between an employer and a union dealing with employee pay, benefits, disciplinary and grievance procedures, and other conditions of employment.

concerted activity. Union organizing activity or other activity by employees for the purpose of bettering wages, hours, or working conditions. Concerted activity is protected by the *National Labor Relations Act.*

consideration. In contract law, the inducements, rights, or things of value that the parties to a contract agree to exchange.

conciliation. A type of alternative dispute resolution, during which parties to a dispute are brought together and encouraged a reach a voluntary agreement settling their differences. In discrimination cases, after the investigative agency—the EEOC or a state or county fair employment practices agency—has reasonable cause to believe discrimination has occurred, the agency may conciliate the charge by working with the parties to develop an appropriate remedy.

constructive discharge. A termination where the employee is forced to quit, either directly or as a result of intolerable working conditions.

consumer report. A credit report and/or an investigative report about a person. The obtaining and use of consumer reports by employers are regulated by the *Fair Credit Reporting Act* and by some state laws.

consumer reporting agency (CRA). A person or entity that, for a fee, regularly assembles or evaluates credit information or other information on consumers for the purpose of furnishing consumer reports to third parties. The obtaining and use of consumer reports from a CRA is regulated by the *Fair Credit Reporting Act* and by some state laws.

contingent worker. A worker who is outside an employer's core workforce of full-time, long-term employees. Contingent workers include independent contractors, part-time employees, job sharers, temporary employees, leased employees, and joint employees.

D

defamation. A false written (libel) or spoken (slander) statement that injures a person's reputation.

direct liability. Liability for an employer's own negligence in hiring, retaining, or failing to supervise an employee who presents an unreasonable risk of injury or damage to the public.

disability. For *Americans with Disabilities Act* purposes, a physical or mental impairment that substantially limits one or more major life activities.

discovery. The formal process by which parties to court proceedings obtain information and documents from opposing parties and question opposing parties and nonparty witnesses under oath.

discrimination. Treating an applicant, an employee, or a group of applicants or employees differently for a reason that is prohibited by law, such as race, color, religion, gender, national origin, age, disability, etc.

disparate impact. In discrimination law, the effect of workplace rules or requirements that appear neutral on their face but that have an adverse impact on a particular race, age group, etc.

disparate treatment. In discrimination law, intentional adverse treatment of an applicant or employee because of his or her race, religion, gender, etc.

domestic partners. Persons other than spouses and relatives who live together and have a voluntary, committed relationship with each other.

due process clause. A clause in the Fifth Amendment to the U.S. Constitution that provides that no person shall be deprived of life, liberty, or property, without due process of law. The Fourteenth Amendment also prohibits states from depriving any person of life, liberty, or property, without due process of law.

E

employee. A person whose manner of work the employer has a right to control.

employee handbook. A handbook of rules, policies, procedures, etc., issued by the employer for the guidance and information of employees.

Employee Polygraph Protection Act (EPPA). The EPPA prohibits employers from using lie detectors except in extremely limited circumstances.

Employer Identification Number (EIN). The number employers obtain from the IRS to use in filing tax returns and reports.

employment contract. An agreement that employment will last for a specific term and/or that the employment will only be terminated for cause or in accordance with specified procedures.

Equal Employment Opportunity Commission (EEOC). The EEOC is the principal enforcer of *Title VII* of the federal *Civil Rights Act*, the *Age Discrimination in Employment Act*, and the employment provisions of the *Americans with Disabilities Act*.

Equal Pay Act. *See Fair Labor Standards Act.*

exempt employee. An employee who is not covered by minimum wage and overtime requirements of the federal *Fair Labor Standards Act* (and the parallel provisions of state law) because he or she is employed in an executive, administrative, or professional capacity or falls within some other statutory exemption.

exit interview. A meeting between an employee and management immediately prior to termination of the employee's employment.

F

Fair Credit Reporting Act (FCRA). The FCRA regulates the obtaining and use of consumer reports.

fair employment practice agency (FEPA). FEPAs, also known as deferral agencies, are state or local agencies that enforce equal employment laws comparable to federal law.

Fair Labor Standards Act (FLSA). The FLSA establishes minimum wages and overtime requirements and prohibits oppressive child labor. As amended by the *Equal Pay Act*, the FLSA also prohibits employers from paying different wages to males and females who do the same work.

False Claims Act. A federal law that permits a whistleblower to file suit in the name of the U.S. Government against companies that have allegedly defrauded the Government.

Family and Medical Leave Act (FMLA). The FMLA requires employers who have fifty or more employees to grant extended leave to employees with serious medical conditions, for the birth or adoption of a child, and when a family member has a serious medical condition.

Federal Arbitration Act (FAA). The FAA provides for enforcement of arbitration agreements.

Federal Insurance Contribution Act (FICA). FICA imposes a tax on employers and an identical tax on employees to fund the Social Security system.

fiduciary. A person who holds a special position of trust with respect to another person, such as the trustee of a pension plan. Fiduciaries are required to act solely in the best interests of the persons for whom they hold the special trust position and not in their own self-interest.

fresh consideration. Something of value, such as a promotion or pay raise, offered to an existing employee in exchange for the employee's signing a non-competition agreement.

Friendship, Commerce, and Navigation Treaties (FCN Treaties). FCN treaties permit foreign companies doing business in the U.S. to engage, at their choice, high-level personnel essential to the functioning of the enterprise, effectively permitting them to discriminate in favor of their own nationals.

frontpay. Pay awarded to an employee or applicant for employment that, but for discrimination, an unfair labor practice, or other wrongful conduct by the employer, would have been earned after the time the award is made.

G

general duty clause. The *Occupational Safety and Health Act* requirement that every employer furnish its employees with employment and a place of employment free from recognized hazards that cause or are likely to cause death or serious physical harm.

general employer. An employer who transfers an employee to another employer (called the special employer) for a limited period of time. While the transfer is in effect, the special employer has temporary responsibility and control over the employee's work.

golden parachute. Payments promised to key personnel in the event of a change in ownership or control of a company.

H

harassment. A form of discrimination involving conduct that has the purpose or effect of unreasonably interfering with a person's work performance or that creates an intimidating, hostile, or offensive work environment.

Health Insurance Portability and Accountability Act (HIPAA). Imposes requirements on group health plans to make it easier for employees who change jobs to be eligible for full coverage under their new employer's plan.

hostile environment. A work environment made offensive by harassment.

human resources (HR). Formerly called personnel.

I

I-9. The form employers must complete and maintain for each employee as a record that the employee is eligible to work in the U.S.

Immigration Reform and Control Act of 1986 (IRCA). An amendment to the *Immigration and Nationality Act*, IRCA prohibits employers from hiring aliens who are ineligible to work in the U.S. IRCA also prohibits discrimination against noncitizens.

independent contractor. A person whose work methods the employer does not have a right to control.

inevitable disclosure. A legal doctrine, adopted in a few states, permitting a court to enjoin a former employee from working for a competitor when the former employee has confidential information and when the old and new jobs are so similar that disclosure of the confidential information is inevitable.

Internal Revenue Code (I.R.C.). The set of laws passed by Congress regarding tax related matters.

involuntary servitude. Slavery or other forms of compulsory work, prohibited by the Thirteenth Amendment to the Constitution and federal law.

L

last chance contract. An agreement between an employer and an employee that gives the employee a final opportunity to conform to company requirements or else be fired.

liquidated damages. In contract law, an amount specified by the parties in advance that a party would be entitled to receive if the other party breaches the contract. While a liquidated damage provision eliminates the need to prove a party's actual damages, the amount of damages specified must be reasonable and cannot be so high as to amount to a penalty that the courts will not enforce.

M

managers only manual. A manual of policies and procedures distributed only to management-level employees.

mass layoff. A layoff of at least 50 employees at a single site that amounts to at least 33% of the workforce at that site.

master-servant relationship. An outdated reference to an employer-employee relationship.

ministerial exception. An exception to laws prohibiting discrimination on the basis of religion. Under the ministerial exception, religious organizations may discriminate in the selection of their clergy.

N

negligent employment. *See direct liability.*

nepotism. The practice of hiring relatives or favoring them in workplace decisions.

noncompete agreement. An agreement that an employee will not compete with his or her former employer after the employment terminates.

nonexempt employee. An employee who is covered by minimum wage and overtime requirements of the *Fair Labor Standards Act* (or the parallel provisions of state law).

O

Occupational Safety and Health Act (OSHA). An act that requires employers to comply with a variety of safety and health standards for the protection of thier employees.

Older Workers Benefit Protection Act (OWBPA). An amendment to the *Age Discrimination in Employment Act*, OWBPA imposes special requirements for releases of ADEA claims in connection with exit incentive programs offered to groups of employees.

open shop. A workplace that employs both union and nonunion employees.

oppressive child labor. With certain exceptions, employment of any child who is under the age of 16, regardless of the occupation, and employment of a child who is between the ages of 16 and 18 in mining, manufacturing, or other hazardous industries.

P

personnel manual. *See employee handbook.*

polygraph. A lie detector. Polygraph tests in connection with employment are generally prohibited.

predatory hiring. A campaign to hire workers away from a particular company in order to harm that company's ability to compete. Predatory hiring may violate antitrust laws.

Pregnancy Discrimination Act (PDA). An amendment to *Title VII* of the federal *Civil Rights Act* that defines sex discrimination to include discrimination because of pregnancy, childbirth, or related medical conditions.

prevailing wage. The wage paid for a particular job category. An employer must obtain a prevailing wage determination as part of the process of applying for an H-1B visa. State and local government contracts sometimes contain provisions requiring contractors to pay their employees prevailing wages.

principal. The person on whose behalf an agent acts.

Professional Employment Organization (PEO). An organization that, for a fee, jointly employs a company's employees in order to provide HR-related functions, such as benefit plan administration, payroll services, and workers' compensation coverage.

progressive discipline. A policy of imposing increasingly severe discipline for repetitive misconduct.

Q

qualifying event. An event that triggers an opportunity to elect COBRA coverage.

quid pro quo. A type of sex discrimination involving sexual favors in exchange for tangible job benefits.

R

Racketeer Influenced and Corrupt Organizations Act (RICO). A 1970 federal statute, primarily aimed at organized crime, that has been applied to employers who repeatedly violate immigration or other laws.

reasonable accommodation. A requirement under the *Americans with Disabilities Act* to protect persons with disabilities. A requirement under *Title VII* of the federal *Civil Rights Act* to allow for employee religious practices.

restrictive covenant. A noncompete agreement. An agreement that an employee will not compete with a former employer after the employment terminates.

respondeat superior. The legal doctrine that imposes vicarious liability on an employer for the negligence of its employees.

retaliation. Taking adverse action against an employee for exercising rights protected by law.

reverse discrimination. Discrimination against members of an historically advantaged group which results from treating members of an historically disadvantaged group more favorably. Quota systems and some affirmative action plans can amount to reverse discrimination.

right-to-work law. A state law that prohibits collective bargaining agreements from containing union security clauses.

S

salt. A person who applies for a job in order to unionize the workplace once hired.

Sarbanes-Oxley Act. Legislation passed by Congress in 2002 in the wake of numerous corporate scandals. The Act makes it criminal for a publicly-traded company to retaliate against an employee who assists in any investigation by federal regulators, Congress, or company supervisors, or who provides information to federal law enforcement officers. Employees who suffer unlawful retaliation may also initiate civil suits for reinstatement, back pay, and other damages.

seniority system. A system followed by management, either by custom or pursuant to a collective bargaining agreement with its unions, under which an employee with greater longevity will be favored for promotion or reassignment over otherwise equally qualified candidates.

special employer. An employer who has borrowed an employee from another employer (called the general employer) for a limited time period and has temporary responsibility and control over the employee's work.

statute of frauds. A provision in state law requiring certain contracts to be in writing to be enforceable in court.

statute of limitations. A provision in law that bars lawsuits that are not filed within a specified time period.

statutory employee. A person who, by law, is classified as an employee for income tax, workers' compensation, or other purposes, even though he or she might otherwise qualify as an independent contractor.

T

tester. A person who applies for a job for the sole purpose of testing the employer's hiring practices for discrimination.

Title VII. The sections of the *Civil Rights Act* that prohibit discrimination in employment.

trade secret. Business information, such as a customer list, formula, or process, that has value because it is not widely known.

U

unemployment insurance. A federal/state system funded by employers, under which employees who have involuntarily lost their jobs receive temporary benefits.

unfair labor practice (ULP). Conduct by an employer or a union that violates the *National Labor Relations Act*.

Uniformed Services Employment and Reemployment Rights Act (USERRA). USERRA requires service members on military leave to continue to be carried as employees for certain benefit and seniority purposes and to be reemployed when they return from military leave.

union security clause. A provision in a collective bargaining agreement that protects union membership or revenue. A union security clause may require that employees be union members in order to be hired (closed shop), that they join a union after being hired (union shop), or that, in the case of nonunion employees, they pay dues as if they were members (agency shop).

union shop. A type of union security arrangement under which employees are required to join a union within a specified time after hire.

United States Citizenship and Immigration Services (USCIS). Part of the U.S. Department of Homeland Security. The USCIS is the successor agency to the Immigration and Naturalization Service of the Department of Justice.

V

vested. Nonforfeitable. When pension plan benefits are vested, they belong to the employee—even if employment ends or the plan is terminated.

vicarious liability. Liability imposed on an employer for the negligence of an employee that occurs in the course of employment.

Vietnam Era Veterans' Readjustment Assistance Act (VEVRAA). VEVRAA prohibits most federal contractors from discriminating against Vietnam-era and disabled veterans and requires affirmative action to ensure equal employment opportunity.

W

W-2. The federal tax form employers issue to employees and also send to the IRS to report wages.

weekly benefit amount (WBA). For unemployment insurance purposes, the amount a claimant is entitled to (but for any disqualification) as determined from his or her base period wages.

whistleblower. An employee who discloses fraud or other wrongdoing by an employer.

Worker Adjustment and Retraining Notification Act (WARN). A federal law that requires employers with 100 or more employees to give 60 days' advance notice of a mass layoff or plant closing.

work-for-hire. A product created or invented by an employee for his or her employer, the copyright or patent rights of which belong to the employer.

wrongful discharge. *See abusive discharge.*

Appendix A:
State Employment
Security Agencies

These agencies develop detailed information about local labor markets, such as current and projected employment by occupation and industry, characteristics of the work force, and changes in state and local area economic activity. Listed below are the Internet addresses of these agencies, as well as addresses and telephone numbers of the directors of research and analysis in these agencies.

Most states have career information delivery systems (CIDS). Look for these systems in secondary schools, postsecondary institutions, libraries, job training sites, vocational rehabilitation centers, and employment service offices. The public can use the systems' computers, printed material, microfiche, and toll free hotlines to obtain information on occupations, educational opportunities, student financial aid, apprenticeships, and military careers. Ask counselors for specific locations. (A listing of state occupational projections also are available on the Internet at **www.projectionscentral.com**.)

Alabama

Chief, Labor Market Information
  Division
Department of Industrial Relations
649 Monroe Street, Room 427
Montgomery, AL 36131-2280
334-242-8859
www.dir.state.al.us/lmi

Alaska

Chief, Research and Analysis Section
Department of Labor and Workforce
  Development
1111 West 8th Street
Juneau, AK 99802-5501
907-465-6035
http://almis.labor.state.ak.us

Arizona

Research Administrator
Department of Economic Security
1789 West Jefferson Street, 733A
Phoenix, AZ 85005-6123
602-542-3871
www.workforce.az.gov

Arkansas

Director, Labor Market Information
Employment Security Department
P.O. Box 2981
Little Rock, AR 72203-2981
501-682-3159
www.state.ar.us/esd

California

Chief, Labor Market Information
    Division, MIC57
Employment Development Department
7000 Franklin Boulevard, Building 1100
Sacramento, CA 95823
916-262-2160
www.calmis.cahwnet.gov

Colorado

Director, Labor Market Information
Department of Labor and Employment
1515 Arapahoe Street, Tower 2
Suite 300
Denver, CO 80202-2117
303-318-8898
http://coworkforce.com/lmi/

Connecticut

Director, Employment Security Division
    Research and Information
Department of Labor
200 Folly Brook Boulevard
Wethersfield, CT 06109-1114
860-263-6255
www.ctdol.state.ct.us/lmi/index.htm

Delaware

Chief, Office of Occupational and
    Labor Market Information
Department of Labor
4425 N. Market Street
Fox Valley Annex
Wilmington, DE 19809-1307
302-761-8050
www.oolmi.net

District of Columbia

Chief, Office of Labor Market Research
    and Information
64 New York Avenue NE
Suite 3035
Washington, D.C. 20002
202-671-1633
http://does.dc.gov/does

Florida

Process Manager, Labor Market
    Statistics
Agency for Workforce Innovation
    MSC G-020
107 E. Madison Street
Tallahassee, FL 32399-4111
850-488-1048
www.labormarketinfo.com

Georgia

Director, Workforce Information
and Analysis
Department of Labor
223 Courtland Street
Room 300
CWC Building
Atlanta, GA 30303
404-232-3875
www.dol.state.ga.us/lem/get_labor_
market_information.htm

Guam

Director, Government of Guam
125 Tun Jesus Crisostomo
Sunny Plaza
2nd Floor
Tamuning, GU 96911
671-647-7066

Hawaii

Chief, Research and Statistics Office
Department of Labor and Industrial
Relations
830 Punchbowl Street, Room 304
Honolulu, HI 96813
808-586-8999
www.state.hi.us/dlir/rs/loihi

Idaho

Chief, Research and Analysis Bureau
Department of Labor
317 Main Street
Boise, ID 83735-0670
208-334-6170
www.labor.state.id.us/lmi/id-lmi.htm

Illinois

Director, Economic Information and
Analysis
Illinois Department of Employment
Security
33 South State Street
9th Floor
Chicago, IL 60603-2802
312-793-2316
http://lmi.ides.state.il.us

Indiana

Director, Labor Market Information—
South E211
Department of Workforce Development
10 North Senate Avenue
Indianapolis, IN 46204-2277
317-232-7460
www.dwd.state.in.us

Iowa

Division Administrator, Information
and Policy Division
Iowa Workforce Development
1000 East Grand Avenue
Des Moines, IA 50319-0209
515-281-0255
www.state.ia.us/iwd

Kansas

Chief, Labor Market Information
Services
Department of Human Resources
401 SW Topeka Boulevard
Topeka, KS 66603-3182
785-296-5058
http://laborstats.hr.state.ks.us

Kentucky

Manager, Research and Statistics
  Branch
Department for Employment Services
WorkforceDevelopment Cabinet
275 East Main Street, 2 W-G
Frankfort, KY 40621
502-564-7976
www.workforcekentucky.ky.gov

Louisiana

Director, Research and Statistics
  Section
Department of Labor
1001 North 23rd Street
Baton Rouge, LA 70804-4094
225-342-3141
www.laworks.net

Maine

Director, Division of Labor Market
  Information Services
Maine Department of Labor
20 Union Street
Augusta, ME 04330-6826
207-287-2271
www.state.me.us/labor/lmis/index.html

Maryland

Director, Labor Market Analysis and
  Information
Department of Labor
Licensing and Regulations
1100 North Eutaw Street
Room 316
Baltimore, Md. 21201-2206
410-767-2250
www.dllr.state.md.us/lmi/index.htm

Massachusetts

Assistant Director for Research
  Division of Employment and Training
19 Staniford Street
Boston, MA 02114
617-626-6556
www.detma.org/LMIHome.htm

Michigan

Director, Labor Market Information
  Division
Department of Career Development
3032 West Grand Boulevard
9th Floor
Detroit, MI 48202
313-456-3090
www.michlmi.org

Minnesota

Labor Market Information Director
Department of Employment
  and Economic Development
390 N. Robert Street
5th Floor
St. Paul, MN 55101
651-296-4087
www.deed.state.mn.us

Mississippi

Chief, Labor Market Information
  Division
Employment Security Commission
1520 West Capitol Street
Jackson, MS 39215-1699
601-961-7424
www.mesc.state.ms.us/lmi/index.html

Missouri

Research Manager, Labor Market
  Information
Department of Economic Development
301 West High Street
Jefferson City, MO 65102
573-751-3609
www.works.state.mo.us/lmi

Montana

Director, Research and Analysis
Department of Labor and Industry
1327 Lockey and Roberts Streets
Helena, MT 59601
406-444-2430
http://rad.dli.state.mt.us

Nebraska

Administrator, Labor Market
  Information Center
Nebraska Workforce Development
550 South 16th Street
Lincoln, NE 68508
402-471-9964
www.dol.state.ne.us/nelmi.htm

Nevada

Chief, Research and Analysis
Department of Employment Training
  and Rehabilitation
500 East Third Street
Carson City, NV 89713-0020
775-684-0387
www://detr.state.nv.us/lmi/index.htm

New Hampshire

Director, Economic and Labor Market
  Information
Department of Employment Security
32 South Main Street
Concord, NH 03301-4587
603-228-4123
www.nhworks.state.nh.us/lmipage.htm

New Jersey

Director, Labor Market and
  Demographic Research
Department of Labor
John Fitch Plaza
5th Floor
Trenton, NJ 08625
609-292-0099
www.state.nj.us/labor/lra

New Mexico

Research Chief, Economic Research
  and Analysis
Department of Labor
501 Mountain Road
Albuquerque, NM 87102
505-841-8645
www.dol.state.nm.us/dol_lmif.html

New York

Director, Division of Research
  and Statistics
New York State Department of Labor
State Campus
Building 12
Room 402
Albany, NY 12240-0020
518-457-6369
www.labor.state.ny.us

North Carolina

Director, Labor Market Information
  Division
Employment Security Commission
700 Wade Avenue
Raleigh, NC 27605
919-733-2936
www.ncesc.com

North Dakota

LMI Director, Research and Statistics
Job Service North Dakota
1000 East Divide
Bismarck, ND 58501
701-328-2868
www.state.nd.us/jsnd/warehouse.htm?
  bookmark=warehouse

Ohio

Director, Labor Market Information
  Division
Department of Job and Family Services
4300 Kimberly Parkway
3rd Floor
Columbus, OH 43232
614-752-9494
http://lmi.state.oh.us

Oklahoma

Director, Economic Research
  and Analysis
Employment Security Commission
2401 N. Lincoln
Room 402-1
Oklahoma City, OK 73105
405-557-7265
www.oesc.state.ok.us/lmi/default.htm

Oregon

Manager, Workforce and Economic
  Research
Oregon Employment Department
875 Union Street, NE
Room 207
Salem, OR 97311-9986
http://olmis.emp.state.or.us

Pennsylvania

Director, Center for Workforce
  Information and Analysis
Department of Labor and Industry
Seventh and Forster Streets
Room 220
Harrisburg, PA 17121-0001
717-787-3266
www.dli.state.pa.us/workforceinfo

Puerto Rico

Director, Bureau of Labor Statistics
Department of Labor and Human
  Resources
505 Munoz Rivera Avenue
17th Floor
Hato Rey, PR 00918
787-754-5340

Rhode Island

Director, Labor Market Information
Department of Employment and
  Training
1511 Pontiac Avenue
Cranston, RI 02920
401-462-8767
www.dlt.ri.gov/lmi

South Carolina

Director, Labor Market Information
  Division
Employment Security Commission
631 Hampton Street
Columbia, SC 29201
803-737-2660
www.sces.org/lmi/index.asp

South Dakota

Director, Labor Market Information
  Division
Department of Labor
420 S. Roosevelt Street
Aberdeen, SD 57401-5131
www.state.sd.us/dol/lmic/index.htm

Tennessee

Director, Research and Statistics
  Division
Department of Labor and Workforce
  Development
500 James Robertson Parkway
11th Floor
Nashville, TN 37245-1000
615-741-2284
www.state.tn.us/labor-wfd/lmi.htm

Texas

Director, Labor Market Information
Texas Workforce Commission
9001 North IH-35, Suite 103A
Austin, TX 75753
512-491-4802
www.tracer2.com

Utah

LMI Director, Workforce Information
Department of Workforce Services
140 East 300 South
Salt Lake City, UT 84111
801-526-9401
http://jobs.utah.gov/wi

Vermont

Chief, Research and Analysis
Department of Employment
  and Training
5 Green Mountain Drive
Montpelier, VT 05602
802-828-4153
www.vtlmi.info

Virgin Islands

Chief, Bureau of Labor Statistics
Department of Labor
53-A, 54 A and B, Kronprindsens Gade
Charlotte Amalie, VI 00801
340-776-3700

Virginia

Director, Economic Information
  Services
Virginia Employment Commission
703 East Main Street
Richmond, VA 23219
804-786-7496
www.vec.state.va.us/index.cfm?loc=
  lbrmkt&info=lmi

Washington

Director, Labor Market and Economic
    Analysis
Employment Security Department
605 Woodland Square Loop
Lacey, WA 98506
360-438-4804
www.wa.gov/esd/lmea

West Virginia

Director, Research Information
    and Analysis Division
Bureau of Employment Programs
112 California Avenue
Room 107
Charleston, WV 25305-0112
304-558-2660
www.state.wv.us/bep/lmi/default.htm

Wisconsin

Director, Bureau of Workforce
    Information
Department of Workforce Development
201 E. Washington Avenue
Madison, WI 53702
608-267-9705
www.dwd.state.wi.us/dwelmi

Wyoming

Manager, Research and Planning
Department of Employment
246 South Center Street
2nd floor
Casper, WY 82601
307-473-3807
http://wydoe.state.wy.us

Appendix B: Outline of Employee Handbook

Employee handbooks must be tailored to each individual employer's situation. One size does not fit all. This appendix includes an outline and brief description (for illustration purposes only) of topics typically covered in an employee handbook.

A disclaimer should be placed prominently on the cover of the handbook stating that:

- the handbook is not a contract of employment;
- it is intended only as a convenient reference for the company's current employment policies;
- the company reserves the right to change its policies at any time without prior notice; and,
- nothing in the handbook is intended to affect the at-will status of any employee or to create or imply a contract of employment.

SECTION 1—INTRODUCTION

A. Definitions

Define specialized words used in the handbook, such as "at-will employment," "employer," "full-time" and "part-time" employees, "employment date" and "employment year," "exempt" and "non-exempt" employees, "regular" and "temporary" employees, "independent contractors," "immediate family" and "termination for cause."

B. Purpose and Scope of Handbook

Describe the handbook as a convenient source of information about the Company and its current policies and procedures, which are intended to promote harmonious, efficient working relationships; to protect the safety and well-being of all employees, and to assure compliance with applicable laws. State the classes of employees to whom the handbook applies. Reserve the right to change or suspend policies and procedures at any time. Include a disclaimer that the handbook is not intended as a contract of employment, it is not intended to grant enforceable rights to any employee, and it is not intended to be a legally binding document.

C. Company Organization and History

Describe the type of entity the Company is—corporation, limited liability company, etc.— and the state where it was formed or organized.

D. Description of Business

Describe the Company's business and the industry and locale in which the Company operates. Unique products, market share, etc. may be mentioned. Relationships with prominent customers may be mentioned if the relationships are likely to endure.

E. Employment Relationship in General

State that the employment relationship between the Company and each employee is an at-will relationship unless the Company and the employee have signed a written employment agreement specifying that the relationship is not at will.

F. Arbitration of Disputes

State Company policy on resolution of employment disputes by arbitration.

G. Unions

Identify any unions involved in representing Company employees.

SECTION 2—HIRING PROCESS

A. Equal Opportunity

State that:

- the Company is an equal opportunity employer;
- the Company does not discriminate in the hiring process or in any aspect of employment; and,
- all employment decisions, both during the hiring process and throughout the employment relationship, are based on merit alone—without regard to race, color, religion, sex, national origin, age, disability, etc.

B. Immigration Status

State that:

- the Company employs only persons who are eligible to work in the United States;
- the Company will not offer employment to, or employ, illegal aliens or other persons who are not eligible to work here;
- persons who are eligible to work will be considered on a non-discriminatory basis regardless of citizenship; and,
- the Company does not have a policy limiting employment to U.S. citizens.

C. Nepotism

State Company policy on hiring relatives of current employees.

D. Application for Employment

State that:

- the Company requires every applicant for employment to complete a written application on the Company's standard form and
- depending on the particular job being applied for, the Company may also require additional items, such as a drug test, credit check, background investigation, criminal convictions check, driver's license and/or driving record, security clearance, etc.

State that providing false or misleading information to the Company in connection with an application for employment is grounds for rejection or dismissal.

E. Procedure Upon Initial Hire or Rehire

Describe the Company's procedure for completing the hiring process. List items and processes that new employees are required to furnish or complete, such as I-9, countersigned copy of offer letter, noncompete and confidentiality agreement, arbitration agreement, physical exam, Form W-4 and state counterpart, direct deposit form, benefit enrollment forms, etc.

F. Directory of New Hires

Inform employees that within 20 days of hire, the Company will file a Report of New Hire for inclusion in the state Directory of New Hires.

SECTION 3—GENERAL OFFICE POLICIES

A. Exclusivity

Describe the Company's policy regarding employment by competitors, owning an interest in a competing company, and moonlighting.

B. Confidentiality and Trade Secrets

Describe the Company's confidentiality policy.

C. Ownership of Intellectual Property

Describe the Company's policy regarding ownership of copyrightable and patentable works.

D. Noncompetition and Nonsolicitation

State whether employees, or certain classes of employees, are required to sign noncompete and nonsolicitation agreements.

E. Insider Trading

Prohibit trading in Company stock, or stock of client companies, based on insider information.

F. Office Hours

State the Company's normal office hours.

G. Meals and Other Breaks

Describe the Company's policy regarding meal and other breaks. Describe any facilities, such as lunch room, subsidized cafeteria, etc., that the Company provides.

H. Holidays

List the holidays the Company normally observes.

I. Dress and Grooming

Describe the Company's dress and grooming policy.

J. Housekeeping

State that the Company requires each employee to maintain his or her work area in a neat, orderly manner and consistent with safety requirements.

K. Fraternization

State Company policy on dating between supervisors and employees and between co-employees.

L. Compliance with Laws

State that employees are expected and required to comply with all laws while on Company business or on the Company's premises. Include, as examples of prohibited activity, gambling, copying proprietary software, dealing in or being under the influence of illegal drugs, discriminating, harassing, submitting false reports to the government, violating health, safety or environmental laws, etc.

M. Time-Keeping

Describe the Company's time-keeping procedures, including particularly the procedures applicable to nonexempt employees.

N. Flex Time

Describe the Company's flex time policy, if any.

O. Work-Sharing

Describe the Company's work-sharing policy, if any.

P. Telecommuting

Describe the Company's telecommuting policy, if any.

Q. Bulletin Board

Describe the Company's bulletin board policy, such as what can be posted, who can post, etc.

SECTION 4—PAY POLICIES

A. Workweek

State the times when the Company's 168-hour workweek begins and ends (for example, Sunday at 12:01 a.m. to 12:00 a.m. the following Saturday).

B. Pay Periods and Payments

State the Company's pay periods and paydays.

C. Overtime Policies

Describe the Company's overtime policies in accordance with the Fair Labor Standards Act and state law.

D. Withholdings and Deductions

Describe the tax and related items withheld from wages, and any other items deducted from wages consistent with state law.

E. Direct Deposit

Describe the Company's direct deposit program.

F. Expenses

Describe the Company's policy regarding authorization to incur business expenses, such as travel, entertainment, etc., and describe the reimbursement procedure, including required documentation.

G. Garnishments and Withholding Orders

Describe the Company's obligations to comply with garnishments and withholding orders, and state any additional policies consistent with federal and state law.

H. Wage Assignments

Describe the Company's policy regarding wage assignments.

SECTION 5—LEAVE POLICIES

A. General

State that the Company reserves the right to change its leave policies from time to time without prior notice.

B. Vacations

Describe the Company's vacation policy as it applies to various classes of employees—regular and temporary, as well as full-time and part-time—including any use-it-or-lose-it policy. Describe the Company's policy on whether accrued vacation is cashed out or lost at termination.

C. Sick Leave

Describe the Company's sick leave policy as it applies to various classes of employees.

D. Extended Leave (FMLA)

Describe the Company's policy regarding extended leave under the *Family and Medical Leave Act* and any state *little FMLA* law, if applicable.

E. Jury Duty, Military Duty, and Attendance in Court

Describe the Company's leave policies in accordance with the *Fair Labor Standards Act* regarding leave for jury duty, military duty, and attendance in court as a witness or crime victim.

F. Military Leave

State the Company's policy regarding continuation of salary and benefits for temporary military service. State that the Company complies with USERRA.

G. Maternity and Paternity Leave

State that the Company treats pregnancy the same as any other temporary disability and will determine whether and to what extent leave will be granted female employees on a case-by-case basis, depending on the employee's medical requirements and the Company's needs. Describe the Company's paternity leave policy.

H. Other Leave

Describe other Company leave policies as they apply to various classes of employees, including whether leave is with or without pay.

SECTION 6—BENEFITS

A. General

State that the Company reserves the right to change its benefits from time to time without prior notice.

B. FICA and Medicare

Describe the Company's withholding and matching obligations under the *Federal Insurance Contribution Act.*

C. Workers' Compensation

Describe the Company's obligations under state workers' compensation law.

D. Unemployment Insurance

Describe the Company's obligations under federal and state unemployment insurance laws.

E. Group Health Insurance

Describe in general terms the Company's group health insurance plan. Refer employees to plan documents, including the Summary Plan Description.

F. Other Benefits

Describe in general terms the Company's other group benefit plans. Refer employees to plan documents, including the Summary Plan Descriptions.

SECTION 7—EVALUATIONS AND SALARY REVIEWS

Describe the Company's policies and practices regarding evaluations and salary reviews.

SECTION 8—DISCIPLINE AND TERMINATION

A. Code of Ethics

Describe the workplace ethics Company employees are required to follow, dealing with matters such as:

- hiring relatives;
- carrying phantom employees;
- borrowing money from subordinate employees, vendors, or customers;
- accepting bribes, kickbacks, expensive gifts, or lavish entertainment from vendors or customers;
- accepting discounts on purchases from vendors or customers that are not offered to the general public;

- falsifying business records, tax returns, or reports to government agencies;
- carrying *off the book* accounts or funds;
- performing paid services for customers on a personal basis outside normal company channels;
- blacklisting employees, customers, or vendors;
- fixing bids or sharing pricing or cost information with competitors; and,
- requiring customers to buy unwanted products in order to get products they do want.

B. Discipline

Describe the Company's discipline practices and procedures. Include a disclaimer that the Company is not obligated to follow stated practices or procedures in any specific case and may, in its discretion, impose any discipline—including dismissal—that the Company deems appropriate.

C. Voluntary Termination

State that the Company requests two-weeks' notice of termination from employees and that the Company will generally, but is not obligated to, give similar notice when the Company is terminating an employee.

D. Severance Pay

Describe the Company's severance pay policy.

E. Exit Interviews

Describe the Company's exit interview requirements and practices; include a disclaimer that the Company, in its discretion, may decide not to conduct an exit interview in specific cases.

F. References and Recommendations

Describe the Company's policy regarding references and recommendations.

SECTION 9—HEALTH AND SAFETY

A. General

Describe the Company's obligations under the General Duty Clause and each employee's obligation to comply with Company health and safety practices.

B. Specific Standards

Identify any specific standards that apply to the Company under the *Occupational Safety and Health Act* and state law.

C. Use of Vehicles

Describe the Company's policies regarding use of Company vehicles, such as who may drive, licencing requirements, who may be a passenger, whether personal use is permitted, etc.

Describe the Company's policy regarding use of personal vehicles for Company business. State that Company vehicles and any personal vehicles used for Company business will be operated and maintained in compliance with all traffic and safety laws, and that no vehicle will be operated while the driver is under the influence of alcohol or drugs.

D. Solicitation and Distribution

Describe the Company's policy, consistent with the National Labor Relations Act, regarding soliciting and distribution of literature during working hours and on Company property.

E. Smoking

Describe the Company's smoking policy, including smoking in vehicles, in accordance with state and local laws.

F. Weapons

Prohibit the possession of dangerous weapons on Company property or while on Company business.

G. Workplace Violence

Describe the Company's disciplinary policy regarding violence or threats of violence by employees against other employees.

H. Visitors

Describe the Company's policy regarding non-employee visitors to the Company's premises.

SECTION 10—DRUGS AND ALCOHOL

A. Drug-Free Workplace Policy

Prohibit the use, possession, manufacture or sale of controlled substances on Company property or while on Company business.

B. Alcohol Policy

State that possession or use of alcohol, or being under the influence of alcohol, on Company property or while on Company business is prohibited.

Describe the Company's policy regarding serving of alcohol at Company functions.

C. Alcohol and Drug Testing

State whether the Company has a testing policy and, if so, describe the policy.

SECTION 11—DISCRIMINATION

A. Non-Discrimination Generally

State that the Company is an equal opportunity employer, that the Company does not discriminate in the hiring process or in any aspect of employment, and that all employment decisions, both during the hiring process and throughout the employment relationship, are based on merit alone. State that decisions are made without regard to race, color, religion, sex, national origin, age, disability, etc. Include as prohibited criteria any criteria listed in state or local law.

B. Equal Pay

State that the Company pays males and females the same for equal work or work of comparable character.

C. Pregnancy, Childbirth, and Related Medical Conditions

State that the Company prohibits discrimination because of pregnancy, childbirth, or medical conditions related to pregnancy, or childbirth, or because a woman is in her child-bearing years or may become pregnant.

State that the Company generally does not require pregnant women to take leave at any particular point in their pregnancy. Also state that the Company does not restrict the type of work a pregnant woman may perform, so long as she remains able to perform the essential functions of her job.

D. Reasonable Accommodation

State that in accordance with the *Americans with Disabilities Act* and state and local law, the Company will reasonably accommodate any employee who, due to disability, requires reasonable accommodation. State that, in general, it is up to the employee to let the Company know that he or she requires reasonable accommodation due to disability.

State that the Company will reasonably accommodate religious custom and practice.

E. Harassment

State that harassment on the basis of race, color, religion, sex, national origin, age, disability, or any other prohibited criterion is illegal discrimination, even if it the harassment does not directly affect a tangible aspect of employment; specifically define sexual harassment.

F. Complaint Procedure

State that any employee who suffers harassment or other discrimination, or who becomes aware of harassment or discrimination against another employee, an applicant for employment, or a customer, client or vendor of the Company, must notify the Company immediately.

Describe the Company's complaint procedures, including any procedure for anonymous complaints.

State that the Company takes all complaints of discrimination seriously and will promptly investigate all complaints. State that although the Company will conduct its investigation as discretely as possible, the Company cannot assure complete confidentiality.

G. Retaliation

State that the Company will not retaliate in any way against any employee who complains about discrimination, who exercises any right granted to him or her under any civil rights or non-discrimination law or regulation, or who furnishes information relating to a discrimination complaint by another employee.

SECTION 12—SECURITY AND PRIVACY

A. Personal Information

Require that personal information concerning employees, such as home address, telephone number, marital status, name changes, names and addresses of dependents, insurance and retirement beneficiaries, and tax withholding information, be kept accurate and up-to-date. State that the Company will not release any personal information to persons outside the Company except as required by law or in an emergency.

State that personal information is kept separate from information relating to job performance, that personal information is not considered for evaluation purposes, promotions, compensation, etc., but that failure to keep personal information up-to-date could adversely affect an evaluation.

B. Company Directory

Describe the Company's policy regarding the content and distribution of Company directories and Web postings of employee bios, and state that for safety reasons, employees may keep home address, home telephone, and family information out of directories.

C. Personnel Files

Describe the Company's policy with regard to employee access to his or her personnel file and his or her right, if any, to obtain copies or to submit statements contesting any negative information in the file.

D. Protected Health Information

Describe the Company's policy regarding access to and use of protected health information.

E. Mail

Prohibit employees from receiving personal mail at the Company. State that any mail received at the Company will be considered business mail and may be opened by authorized Company personnel.

F. Personal Use of Computer Equipment and Communications Facilities

State that employee telephone conversations, e-mails, and Internet activity are subject to monitoring by the Company at any time. Also state that an employee's desk and office; any other Company space that an employee uses; any mail that an employee receives at the Company; an employee's Company compute;, and, any other Company areas, equipment, facilities and vehicles that an employee uses or that are assigned to an employee, are subject to inspection by the Company at any time.

G. Company Monitoring and Inspection Rights

State that all communications sent or received via the Company's communications facilities, or created by or stored in the Company's communications facilities, or computer equipment belong to the Company, that employees should have no expectation of privacy while at any Company facility, while on Company business, or while using or accessing the Company's computer equipment or communications facilities. Also state that the Company reserves the right to monitor conversations, expect e-mails and other computer files and track Internet usage, including websites visited.

H. Software

State that the Company strictly observes all copyright laws and licensing agreements when acquiring and installing software on Company computers. Prohibit the modification or copying of Company-installed software and prohibit the downloading or installing of personal software on Company computers without express authorization.

I. Inappropriate Use of Computer Equipment and Communications Facilities

Prohibit inappropriate use of Company computer equipment and communications facilities. This includes downloading or transmitting pornography, gambling, violating copyright laws by downloading music or other electronic data without authorization, using another employee's password, spamming, etc.

J. Lie Detectors (Polygraphs)

State that the Company will never request an employee or applicant for employment to submit to a lie detector (polygraph) test and that the Company prohibits use of lie detectors in connection will any aspect of employment by the Company.

L. Cash and Other Valuables

Describe Company policy for safeguarding and depositing receipts.

M. Personal Use of Supplies

State that the Company maintains supplies for the conduct of Company business and that personal use of Company supplies is prohibited.

N. Personal Property

Warn employees that the Company's insurance policy does not cover theft or damage of valuables that employees may bring to the workplace, such as personal laptops, PDAs, etc.

Appendix C: State New Hire Reporting Agencies

The Office of Child Support Enforcement of the U.S. Department of Health and Human Services maintains a list of state new hir reporting information, which is set out in this appendix. (For more information, go to **www.acf.hhs.gov/programs/cse/newhire/employer/ private/index.htm**.)

Alabama

334-353-8491
www.newhire@dir.state.al.us

Alaska

907-269-6089
877-269-6685 *(Alaska only)*
www.csed.state.ak.us/employers/
    employerinformation.htm

Arizona

888-282-2064 *(new hire)*
602-340-0555 *(new hire)*
602-252-4045 *(child support)*
www.az-newhire.com

Arkansas

800-259-2095
501-376-2125
www.ar-newhire.com

California

916-657-0529
www.edd.ca.gov/taxrep/txner.htm

Colorado

800-696-1468
303-297-2849
www.newhire.state.co.us

Connecticut

860-263-6310 *(new hire)*
800-228-5437 *(child support)*
www.ctnewhires.com

Delaware

302-326-6024, ext 188
www.state.de.us/dhss/dcse/page3.html

District of Columbia

877-846-9523
www.new-hires.com/dc

Florida

888-854-4791 (*new hire*)
850-656-3343 (*new hire*)
888-854-4791 (*customer service*)
www.fl-newhire.com

Georgia

888-541-0469
404-525-2985
www.ga-newhire.com

Guam

671-475-3360
www.guamcse.net

Hawaii

808-692-7029
www.state.hi.us/csea/newhire.html

Idaho

800-627-3880
208-332-8941
www.jobservice.us/newhire

Illinois

800-327-HIRE [4473] (*new hire*)
312-793-0322 (*new hire*)
312-793-9856 (*technical information*)
www.ides.state.il.us/employer/newhire/
    general.htm

Indiana

866-879-0198
317-612-3028 (*Indianapolis metro area*)
www.in.gov
www.in-newhire.com

Iowa

515-281-5331
https://secure.dhs.state.ia.us/epics

Kansas

888-219-7801
785-296-5025
www.hr.state.ks.us/home-html/newhires.htm

Kentucky

800-817-2262
www.new-hires.com/ky

Louisiana

888-223-1461
225-342-4591
www.dss.state.la.us/html/new_hire_registry.html

Maine

800-845-5808 (*in-state only*)
207-624-7880
800-442-6003 (*child support*)
www.state.me.us/dhs/bfi/dser/New_Hire.htm

Maryland

410-281-6000 (*customer service*)
www.mdnewhire.com

Massachusetts

617-626-4154 (*new hire info and technical support*)
www.cse.state.ma.us/programs/newhire/
    nh_temp.htm

Michigan

800-524-9846
www.new-hires.com/mi

Minnesota

800-672-4473
651-227-4661
www.mn-newhire.com

Mississippi

800-241-1330
404-808-9016
www.new-hires.com/mississippi

Missouri

800-585-9234 *(employer hot line)*
573-526-8699 *(employer hot line)*
800-859-7999 *(gen. info)*
www.dss.state.mo.us/cse/newhire.htm

Montana

888-866-0327
406-444-9290
www.state.mt.us/revenue/css/3forbusinesses/
    08newhire.asp

Nebraska

888-256-0293 *(new hire)*
402-691-9957 (new hire)
402-479-5555 (child support)
www.NEnewhire.com

Nevada

888-639-7241
775-684-8685
775-687-4487 *(technical info)*
www.welfare.state.nv.us/child/newhires.htm
    #newhire

New Hampshire

800-803-4485
603-229-4371
www.nhes.state.nh.us

New Jersey

888-624-6339
877-NJ HIRES [654-4737]
609-689-1900
www.nj-newhire.com

New Mexico

888-878-1607
505-995-8230
800-288-7207 *(in NM child support info)*
800-585-7631 *(outside NM child support info)*
www.nm-newhire.com

New York

800-972-1233
www.tax.state.ny.us/wt/newhire.htm

North Carolina

888-514-4568 (new hire)
919-877-1011 *(new hire)*
919-874-0092 *(technical support)*
www.ncnewhires.com

North Dakota

800-755-8530 *(in-state only)*
701-328-3582
www.childsupportnd.com

Ohio

888-872-1490
614-221-5330
www.oh-newhire.com

Oklahoma

800-317-3785
405-557-7133
405-557-7297 *(technical info.)*
www.oesc.state.ok.us\newhire

Oregon

503-378-2868 *(accepts collect calls)*
www.dcs.state.or.us/employers.htm

Pennsylvania

888-PAHIRES [724-4737]
www.panewhires.com

Puerto Rico

787-767-1500
(no Web address available)

Rhode Island

888-870-6461 *(new hire info)*
401-222-2847 *(child support info)*
www.RInewhire.com

South Carolina

888-454-5294 *(new hire)*
www.state.sc.us/dss/csed/newhire.htm

South Dakota

888-827-6078
605-626-2942
www.state.sd.us/dol

Tennessee

888-715-2280
615-884-2828
www.tnnewhire.com

Texas

888-TEXHIRE [839-4473] *(new hire)*
800-252-8014 *(child support)*
www.newhire.org/tx

Utah

800-222-2857 *(in-state only)*
801-526-4361
http://jobs.utah.gov/newhire

Vermont

800-786-3214 *(child support)*
www.det.state.vt.us

Virgin Islands

340-776-3700, ext. 2038
(no Web address available)

Virginia

800-979-9014
804-771-9733
www.va-newhire.com

Washington

800-562-0479 *(new hire)*
800-591-2760 *(empl. ombudsman)*
360-586-4357 *(technical support)*
www.wa.gov/dshs/newhire

West Virginia

877-625-4669 *(new hire)*
304-346-9513
www.wv-newhire.com

Wisconsin

888-300-4473
www.dwd.state.wi.us/uinh

Wyoming

800-970-9258
307-638-1675 *(within Laramie County)*
www.wy-newhire.com

Index

childbirth, 37

counting employees, 28, 29, 30

laws, 6, 9, 13, 20, 25, 26, 27, 30, 31, 48, 82, 101, 107, 130

pregnancy, 37

related medical condition, 37

procedures and remedies, 47

remedies, 49, 51

specific types, 33

discriminatory intent, 25

disparate impact, 26, 60

disparate treatment, 26

diversity, 61

documentation, 136

drugs, 40, 41, 88, 137

dual filed, 47

duties, 25, 55, 96

describing, 57

duty of loyalty, 102, 138, 224

E

earned income credit (EIC), 122, 123, 124, 125, 126

earned rate, 227

Eckard Brandes, Inc. v. Riley, 225

Economic Espionage Act, 105

EEOC, 4, 17, 47, 48, 49, 51, 84, 88, 89, 107, 108, 209, 219

Enforcement Guidance, 10

filing a charge, 47

Form 131, 48

processing a charge, 48

Elliott v. Williams, 67

employee handbooks, 87, 97, 98, 99, 137

Employee Polygraph Protection Act (EPPA), 90

Employee Retirement Income Security Act (ERISA), 29, 168, 170, 171, 199

Employee Verification Service, 127

employee's background, 67

employment agencies, 59

Employment and Training Administration, 57

employment application, 70, 76

employment at will. *See at-will employment.*

employment contracts, 67, 93, 96

contents, 96

restrictions on termination, 137

employment guidelines, 86

employment in a family business, 13

employment law, 70

employment of a child, 13, 14

employment relationship, 85, 101

employment-related, 25

Empowerment Zone Employment Credit, 3

equal employment, 97

About the Author

Charles H. Fleischer has an undergraduate degree in political science from the University of Rochester in New York and a law degree (with honors) from the George Washington University in Washington, D.C. He is admitted to practice in Maryland and the District of Columbia, and is a member of the law firm of Oppenheimer, Fleischer & Quiggle, P.C., Bethesda, Maryland. The firm's website is **www.OFQLaw.com**.

Fleischer was a principal author of the employer's petition for writ of certiorari and of the merits briefs in *Meritor Savings Bank v. Vinson*, the first Supreme Court case dealing with sexual harassment. He has advised numerous businesses and associations on employment law issues and he writes and speaks extensively on the topic.

Fleischer lives with his wife in Potomac, Maryland.